Greater Mekong Subregion:

Malaria Operational Plan FY 2014

TABLE OF CONTENTS

ABBREVIATIONS

ACT	artemisinin-based combination therapy
AusAID	Australian Agency for International Development
BCC	behavior change communication
BMGF	Bill and Melinda Gates Foundation
BVBD	Bureau of Vector-Borne Diseases (Thailand)
CDC	U.S. Centers for Disease Control and Prevention
CMPE	Centre for Malaria, Parasitology, and Entomology (Lao People's Democratic Republic)
CMS	Central Medical Store
CMSD	Central Medical Store Depot (Burma)
CNM	National Centre for Parasitology, Entomology, and Malaria (Cambodia)
DFID	UK Department for International Development
DHA-Pip	dihydroartemisinin-piperaquine
FETP	Field Epidemiology Training Program
G6PD	glucose-6-phosphate dehydrogenase
GHI	Global Health Initiative
Global Fund	Global Fund to Fight AIDS, Tuberculosis, and Malaria
GMS	Greater Mekong Sub-Region
HMIS	health management information system
IEC	information, education, communication
IPTp	intermittent preventive treatment for pregnant women
IRS	indoor residual spraying
ITN	insecticide-treated net
JICA	Japan International Cooperation Agency
Lao PDR	Lao People's Democratic Republic
LLIHN	long-lasting insecticide-treated hammock net
LLIN	long-lasting insecticide-treated net
MARC	Myanmar Artemisinin Resistance Containment Project
M&E	monitoring and evaluation
MIS	Malaria Indicator Survey
MMP	Mekong Malaria Programme
MMW	mobile malaria worker
MOH	Ministry of Health
MOP	Malaria Operational Plan
MOPH	Ministry of Public Health (Thailand)
NGO	non-governmental organization
NIMPE	National Institute for Malariology, Parasitology, and Entomology (Vietnam)
NMCP	National Malaria Control Program
OD	operational district
OR	operations research
PMI	President's Malaria Initiative
PSI	Population Services International
QA	quality assurance
QC	quality control

RBM	Roll Back Malaria
RDMA	Regional Development Mission Asia
RDT	rapid diagnostic test
SEARO	Southeast Asia Regional Office
TES	therapeutic efficacy studies
UNICEF	United Nations Children's Fund
USAID	United States Agency for International Development
USG	United States Government
USP	United States Pharmacopeia
VBDC	Vector-borne Disease Control Program (Burma)
WPRO	Western Pacific Regional Office
WHO	World Health Organization

EXECUTIVE SUMMARY

Malaria prevention and control are major foreign assistance objectives of the U.S. Government (USG). In May 2009, President Barack Obama announced the Global Health Initiative (GHI), a comprehensive effort to reduce the burden of disease and promote healthy communities and families around the world. Through the GHI, the United States will help partner countries improve health outcomes, with a particular focus on improving the health of women, newborns, and children.

The President's Malaria Initiative (PMI) is a core component of the GHI, along with HIV/AIDS and tuberculosis. PMI was launched in June 2005 as a five-year, $1.2 billion initiative to rapidly scale up malaria prevention and treatment interventions and reduce malaria-related mortality by 50% in 15 high-burden countries in sub-Saharan Africa. With passage of the 2008 Lantos-Hyde Act, funding for PMI was extended and, as part of the GHI, the goal of PMI was adjusted to reduce malaria-related mortality by 70% in the original 15 countries by the end of 2015. In addition, PMI will work to limit the spread of antimalarial drug resistance in two USAID-supported regional programs, the Mekong Regional Initiative in six Southeast Asian countries and the Amazon Malaria Initiative in seven South American countries.

In line with the 2009 Lantos-Hyde Malaria Strategy, PMI support extends to the Greater Mekong Sub-Region (GMS), which is made up of six countries: Burma, Cambodia, China (Yunnan Province), Lao People's Democratic Republic, Thailand, and Vietnam. Although considerable progress has been made in malaria control in the GMS during the past 10 years, malaria remains a major concern for the international community, ministries of health, and the people of the region. This is due primarily to the development and possible spread of resistance to artemisinin drugs, the principal component of the combination therapies for malaria that now are the first-line treatment for malaria throughout the GMS and the world. *Plasmodium falciparum* resistance to artemisinin drugs has now been confirmed in western Cambodia; failures in artemisinin-based combination therapy (ACT) have been reported from multiple sites on the Thai-Cambodian border; and an early warning sign of artemisinin resistance - prolongation of parasite clearance times - has been reported from the Thailand-Burma and Burma-China borders and in southern Vietnam.

The USG has supported malaria control efforts in the GMS since 2000. These regional efforts have focused on antimalarial drug resistance monitoring and drug quality surveillance. All countries in the GMS have Global Fund to Fight AIDS, Tuberculosis, and Malaria (Global Fund) support. Burma and Cambodia received Round 9 Global Fund malaria grants, and Thailand's Round 10 malaria grant has been approved. The other major source of funding for artemisinin resistance containment in Burma is the multi-donor initiative, Three Millennium Development Goal Fund, formerly known as the Three Diseases Fund. In addition, Global Fund announced a new three-year $100 million initiative for regional efforts to reduce malaria transmission and respond to resistance in GMS countries.

The FY 2014 PMI Malaria Operational Plan for the GMS was developed with the Regional Development Mission for Asia (RDMA), and Burma and Cambodia USAID Missions during a planning visit in April 2013 by representatives from USAID, the Centers for Disease Control and

Prevention, and the national malaria control programs of Burma, Thailand and Cambodia, with the participation of other major partners working on malaria in the area.

The PMI GMS program focuses control efforts in areas of known or emerging artemisinin resistance. The FY 2014 Malaria Operational Plan supports regional/cross-cutting activities, such as surveillance for antimalarial drug resistance and antimalarial drug quality monitoring, and malaria prevention and control activities to reduce malaria transmission in geographically-focused cross-border areas with emerging artemisinin resistance. Original key cross-border focus areas were centered on Tanintharyi-Ranong border areas of Burma and Thailand and the Trat/Chanthaburi-Pailin border areas of Thailand and Cambodia. PMI also supports expanding malaria control activities to other target areas within the three focus countries where there is evidence of confirmed or emerging artemisinin resistance including Kayin and southern Rakhine States in Burma; certain operational districts in Cambodia bordering Thailand, Laos and Vietnam; and Tak and Kanchanaburi Provinces in Thailand. PMI will also consider emergency assistance, including commodity support and technical assistance for surveillance, behavior change communication (BCC), and case management in other GMS areas threatened by artemisinin resistance. The proposed FY 2014 PMI activities are in line with the national malaria control program strategies of the six countries and are intended to complement ongoing Global Fund malaria grants, containment specific projects, and contributions from other donors.

Vector control: Malaria transmission in the GMS is closely associated with two malaria vectors that inhabit the forest and forest fringe, *Anopheles dirus* and *An. minimus*. Countries have made progress in monitoring vector distribution and insecticide resistance, which is not a major problem in the GMS area. Most studies suggest that insecticide-treated nets (ITNs) provide protection even with significant outdoor and early evening biting. There is a strong culture of bed net use in the GMS and net ownership is quite high, especially in Burma and Cambodia, but many of those nets are untreated. Considerable numbers of long-lasting ITNs targeted for townships along the borders between Burma and Thailand and Thailand and Cambodia are included in their respective Global Fund grants. With FY 2011 funding, PMI procured and distributed approximately 230,000 LLINs in focal area in Burma. With FY 2012 funding, PMI procured 145,000 ITNs for Burma, Lao PDR and Cambodia to fill gaps. In addition, 110,000 ITNs were provided to Thailand to cover migrants in 26 provinces in FY 2012. In FY 2013, PMI is procuring 325,000 ITNs for distribution in the PMI cross-border focus areas protecting vulnerable migrant and mobile populations.

With FY 2014 funding, PMI will procure approximately 506,000 LLINs/ hammock nets to fill gaps in Global Fund grants in the cross-border focus areas identified above and develop innovative BCC approaches to improve use. PMI will also provide support to entomological services and training in the region, in response to the changing vector ecology, with a focus on migrant populations and interruption of outdoor transmission. Indoor residual spraying (IRS) is mostly limited to outbreak response and focal control and is not a key activity in national malaria control strategies for any of the GMS countries. Therefore, no PMI funds will be targeted for IRS in the sub-region.

Malaria in Pregnancy: While intermittent preventive treatment for pregnant women (IPTp) is not part of national policies for any country in the sub-region, PMI will support promotion of universal LLIN coverage and prompt diagnosis and treatment of clinical cases of malaria in pregnant women as they remain a vulnerable group in the region. With FY 2011 funding, PMI supported a rapid assessment of malaria in pregnancy to identify programmatic areas for strengthening in focus countries. Building on this assessment's findings and recommendations, PMI will support national programs with updating policies, guidelines, training and supervision materials to strengthen malaria case management and prevention activities provided through antenatal clinics.

Case management: In all countries making up the GMS, diagnosis of malaria is based on laboratory tests with microscopy or rapid diagnostic tests (RDTs), particularly at community level. Although all countries in the sub-region recommend ACTs as the first-line treatment of *P. falciparum* infections, artemisinin resistance has been confirmed on the Thai-Cambodian border and early evidence of developing resistance has been reported from several other sites in the sub-region. Case management of malaria in the GMS is further complicated by the fact that *P. vivax* and *P. falciparum* are both relatively common. Chloroquine is the drug of choice for the treatment of *P. vivax* infections except for Cambodia, although reports of *P. vivax* resistance to chloroquine are emerging from the sub-region. Another problem in the sub-region is the widespread availability of counterfeit and substandard antimalarial drugs, especially artemisinin drugs, and artemisinin monotherapy. With USG support, considerable progress has been made in recent years in establishing effective drug quality monitoring in the sub-region but, to date, engagement with Burma and China has been limited. With FY 2012 funding, PMI procured 238,500 RDTs for the Burma focus areas and 24,000 RDTs and 25 microscopes for targeted operational districts in Cambodia. Over the last year, PMI supported training of community health volunteers and health facility staff in Burma, Cambodia and Thailand in malaria case management including diagnostic testing.

Rapid diagnostic test and ACT needs in Burma, Cambodia, and Thailand are anticipated to be met by those countries' Global Fund grants; however, stock outs have been happening more frequently due to bottlenecks in Global Fund procurement. With FY 2014 funding, PMI will procure small quantities of RDTs to fill gaps and strengthen laboratory capacity in the cross-border focus areas. The PMI will also procure ACT treatments to fill any gaps in Burma and Cambodia and respond to urgent needs in the region. Because of concerns about the quality of malaria diagnosis and treatment in these border areas, PMI will support in-service training and quality assurance of the parasitological diagnosis of malaria. In addition, PMI will continue support to national pharmaceutical reference laboratories to ensure they have the capacity to carry out pre- and post-marketing surveillance of drug quality.

Monitoring and evaluation (M&E), Surveillance and Operational Research: The quality of malaria case detection and reporting systems varies widely within the GMS. In the context of malaria elimination, timely reporting can inform policy decision and focus resources towards outbreak areas or in geographical regions harboring resistant malaria strains. USG funding for M&E during the past several years has focused on building a regional malaria M&E framework, updating national M&E plans, providing technical assistance for surveys, and capacity development at the national level. With FY 2012 and FY 2013 funding, PMI supported surveillance system evaluations in Burma and Laos, providing technical assistance for national surveys in Cambodia and Burma, strengthening routine surveillance systems, and implementing partners collected routine surveillance and survey data at the community level.

With FY 2014 funding, PMI will focus efforts within the cross-border focus areas to implement systems and practices to foster timely collection of quality surveillance and periodic survey data. At the national level, PMI will help all national malaria control programs develop one national M&E plan, support national/ sub-national malaria surveys, and build M&E capacity within their national programs. In Cambodia and Burma where most patients seek care in the private sector, PMI will begin collecting malaria data from private providers. The PMI will continue to support drug resistance monitoring at 24 sites in all six GMS countries. Entomologic surveillance will focus geographically on cross-border areas and operations research will continue to identify vector control interventions appropriate for outdoor transmission settings.

The FY 2014 GMS budget in the amount of $14 million is allocated across countries as follows: $6.5 million to Burma, $4.5 million to Cambodia, and $3 million to Thailand, Lao People's Democratic Republic, and Vietnam.

INTRODUCTION

Malaria prevention and control are major foreign assistance objectives of the U.S. Government (USG). In May 2009, President Barack Obama announced the Global Health Initiative (GHI), a comprehensive effort to reduce the burden of disease and promote healthy communities and families around the world. Through the GHI, the United States will help partner countries improve health outcomes, with a particular focus on improving the health of women, newborns, and children.

The President's Malaria Initiative (PMI) is a core component of the GHI, along with HIV/AIDS and tuberculosis. PMI was launched in June 2005 as a five-year, $1.2 billion initiative to rapidly scale up malaria prevention and treatment interventions and reduce malaria-related mortality by 50% in 15 high-burden countries in sub-Saharan Africa. With passage of the 2008 Lantos-Hyde Act, funding for PMI was extended and, as part of the GHI, the goal of PMI was adjusted to reduce malaria-related mortality by 70% in the original 15 countries by the end of 2015. In addition, PMI will work to limit the spread of antimalarial drug resistance in two USAID-supported regional programs, the Mekong Regional Initiative in six Southeast Asian countries and the Amazon Malaria Initiative in seven South American countries.

Through GHI and PMI, the USG is committed to working closely with host governments and within existing national malaria control plans. Efforts are coordinated with other national and international partners, including the Global Fund to Fight AIDS, Tuberculosis and Malaria (Global Fund), Roll Back Malaria (RBM), the World Bank Malaria Booster Program, and the non-governmental and private sectors, to ensure that investments are complementary and that RBM and Millennium Development Goals are achieved.

Malaria Operational Plan

This FY 2014 Malaria Operational Plan (MOP) presents a detailed implementation plan for the Greater Mekong Sub-Region (GMS), comprising six countries: Burma, Cambodia, China (Yunnan Province), Lao People's Democratic Republic (PDR), Thailand, and Vietnam. It was developed in consultation with the Burma, Thailand and Cambodian National Malaria Control Programs (NMCPs) and with the input of multiple national and international partners involved with malaria prevention and control in the sub-region. The activities that PMI is proposing to support with FY 2014 funding contribute to the countries' national malaria control strategies and plans, and build on malaria investments made by the USG in the sub-region since 2000.

The PMI GMS program differs from PMI's support to malaria programs in Africa both in its regional focus and its primary goal to assist containment of artemisinin resistance. PMI GMS recognizes the original intent of its engagement in the region is due to evidence of artemisinin resistance; as a response to this problem, PMI's strategy is to focus its malaria control and prevention efforts in selected geographic areas with emerging artemisinin resistance along the Thai-Cambodia and Thai-Burmese borders.

The FY 2014 Malaria Operational Plan (MOP) for the GMS includes support to both regional/cross-cutting activities, such as surveillance for antimalarial drug resistance, antimalarial drug quality monitoring, and regional capacity building, as well as targeted malaria prevention and control activities with a country-specific focus. (See Goals and Targets of PMI in GMS for detailed discussion on PMI strategy and objectives.)Support for prevention and control activities in the GMS includes distribution of long-lasting ITNs (LLINs) to protect against indoor biting mosquitoes; testing interventions for those at risk of outdoor transmission; behavior change communication (BCC) to reinforce personal protection as well as appropriate case management in private and public sectors; entomological monitoring to identify when and where infective bites occur; and surveillance for antimalarial drug quality and therapeutic efficacy, especially in areas with emerging artemisinin resistance.

The regional, cross-cutting activities will benefit all six countries making up the GMS, depending on access and other sources of funding. Country-level work plans will be developed for Burma, Thailand and Cambodia to ensure that activities are coordinated for achievement of maximum impact. Given the burden of malaria and the threat of artemisinin resistance in the GMS, the focus of the country-specific, community intervention activities was centered on the Tanintharyi-Ranong border areas of Burma and Thailand and the Trat/Chanthaburi-Pailin border areas of Thailand and Cambodia. Although these selected cross-border focus areas are the geographic areas in the GMS of greatest concern for artemisinin resistance, there are emerging sites along the Burma-Thailand and Cambodia-Thailand borders with resistance. Therefore, PMI also supports expanding malaria control activities to other target areas within the three focus countries where there is evidence of confirmed or emerging artemisinin resistance including: Kayin and Rakhine States in Burma; Tak and Kanchanaburi provinces in Thailand; and certain operational districts in Cambodia bordering Thailand, Laos and Vietnam. In coordination with NMCP strategies and other donor efforts, PMI will concentrate its commodity investments as well as additional M&E resources in the cross-border focus areas to ensure access to quality malaria prevention and curative services. Commodity support will aim to fill gaps in all cross-border focus areas, but the need is likely to be greatest in Burma.

This document briefly reviews the current status of malaria control policies and interventions in the GMS, describes progress to date, identifies challenges and unmet needs if the targets of the NMCPs and PMI are to be achieved, and provides a description of planned activities with FY 2014 funding.

NATIONAL MALARIA CONTROL PROGRAMS[1] AND THE MALARIA SITUATION

GMS

Malaria control in the GMS faces many challenges different from those in the African context. The sub-region is the epicenter of the world's most severe drug resistance with chloroquine resistance developing in the late 1950s, followed by resistance to sulfadoxine-pyrimethamine, mefloquine, and decreased sensitivity to quinine. The emergence of artemisinin resistance on the Thai-Cambodia border, the same area where chloroquine resistance emerged 50 years ago, is of

---

[1]Malaria in the Greater Mekong Subregion: Regional and Country Profiles. WHO 2010

great concern as this is the last remaining efficacious antimalarial drug for *Plasmodium falciparum* worldwide. Beyond drug resistance, NMCPs in the sub-region face several related challenges including a vibrant private sector with an abundance of sub-standard and counterfeit medicines, migrant and mobile populations, vulnerable and remotely settled ethnic minorities, poor public health infrastructure, weak surveillance and M&E systems, civil strife, and occasional cross-border conflicts.

The key malaria control strategies and policies of the countries comprising the GMS are listed in Table 2.[2] All countries in the GMS now recommend ACTs for first-line treatment of *Plasmodium falciparum.*

Table 1. Key national strategies and policies in malaria control

	Burma	Cambodia	China	Lao PDR	Thailand	Vietnam
Year treatment/ diagnosis guidelines most recently updated	2008	2012	2009	2011	2011	2009
First-line treatment for *P. falciparum*	AL; AS+M; DHA-Pip	DHA-Pip; AS+M; AP in Pailin	DHA-Pip; AS+AQ; ART+ naphthoquine; ART+PIP (Pip monotherapy as chemoprophylaxis)	AL	DHA-Pip AP (Zone 1)	DHA-Pip
Anti-gametocytocidal treatment	45 mg PQ	45 mg PQ with testing or when safety data available			30 mg PQ	30 mg PQ
First-line treatment for *P. vivax*	CQ+PQ	DHA-Pip + PQ 45mg/wk x 8 wks.	CQ+PQ	AL	CQ+PQ	CQ+PQ
Number of antimalarial drug resistance monitoring sites:	10	5	3 (currently inactive)	3	9	5
Number of insecticide resistance monitoring sites:	1	4	N/A	10	2	>10
AL- artemether-lumefantrine; AS- artesunate; M- mefloquine; DHA- dihydroartemisinin; Pip- piperaquine; CQ- chloroquine; PQ- primaquine; AQ- amodiaquine; AP- Atovaquone- proguanil; SP- sulfadoxine-pyrimethamine						

---

[2] Malaria in the Greater Mekong Subregion: Regional and Country Profiles. WHO 2010

The malaria situation across the GMS is very complex and ranges from countries on track for malaria elimination to countries that are just beginning to scale-up malaria control activities. Unlike most sub-Saharan African countries, the GMS must contend with multiple parasite species, with *P. vivax* more prevalent in some countries, and most importantly, multi-drug resistance. Furthermore, at least 10 species of anopheline mosquitoes are involved in malaria transmission in the GMS. Primary vectors can be *An. dirus*, *An. minimus* and/or *An. maculatus*, numerous vector species are not endophilic (bite within structures), and vector status and relative importance can change with location and season. Much of the malaria burden in the sub-region is concentrated along border areas and in forest or forest-fringe areas where the region's most efficient vector, *An. dirus*, exists. Approximately, three-quarters of the reported cases in the GMS occur in Burma. The annual figures shown in the table below reported by the NMCPs to World Health Organization (WHO)for the sub-region probably under-estimate the true burden of malaria as it captures data only from the public sector.

Table 2. Malaria burden in the GMS (public sector data)

	Estimated population in malaria endemic (high + low risk) areas (millions)	Probable and confirmed malaria cases	Confirmed cases	Percent falciparum	Inpatient malaria deaths	Artemisinin resistance (suspected and confirmed)
Burma	29	567,452	465,294	67.3	581	Suspected (eastern border)
Cambodia*	3.3	74,592	70,454	37.0	45	Confirmed (western border)
China	563.6	4,498	3,367	41.8	33	Suspected (Yunnan)
Laos	3.7	17,904	17,835	92.9	17	None detected
Thailand	34.8	24,897	24,897	39.9	43	Confirmed (west and east borders)
Viet Nam	33.3	45,588	16,612	64.3	14	Confirmed in Binh Phuoc and suspected in Gia Lai
Source: WMR 2012; *2012 NMCP data						

Over the past decade, GMS countries have made tremendous progress in reducing the number of malaria cases and deaths. From 1998 to 2010, the six countries have collectively reported an 81% reduction in the annual number of deaths attributed to malaria. Multiple factors have contributed to this reduction. Governments and partners have made malaria control a priority by increasing investments, successfully garnering international funding, strengthening political will, integrating malaria control efforts into national health systems, and intensifying cross-border collaboration. It is also likely that environmental changes such as deforestation, economic development, demographic stabilization, greater political stability, and improved coverage of basic health services have impacted malaria morbidity and mortality in the GMS.[7]

The most important new development for malaria control in GMS concerns donor funding, especially from the Australian Agency for International Development(AusAID), the Bill and Melinda Gates Foundation (BMGF), and the Global Fund. Following on-the-ground, joint assessments of efforts to control artemisinin resistance, AusAID drew attention to significant funding and implementation gaps and invited senior regional health officials to a conference entitled "Malaria 2012: Saving Lives in the Asia-Pacific," in Sydney, Australia. Further Australian assistance was announced, totaling $50 million for three years, including $25 million for GMS; both AusAID and BMGF used these funds to assist WHO to establish a regional "hub" in Phnom Penh, Cambodia, in support of WHO's plan for Emergency Response to Artemisinin Resistance. The Global Fund then announced a special three-year $100 million initiative for regional efforts to reduce malaria transmission and respond to resistance. The upshot of these initiatives is increased international attention to malaria control and artemisinin resistance, as well as greatly increased funding; however, constraints of weak systems and inadequate human resources remain. PMI works closely with development partners to maximize effective use of all available resources.

Burma

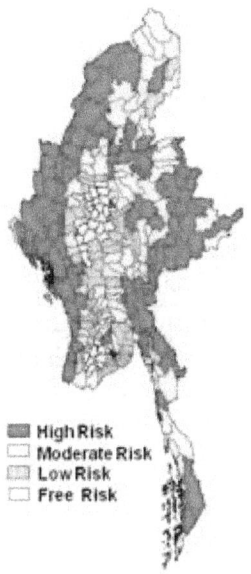

Among the six Mekong countries, the malaria burden is highest in Burma, where it remains a leading cause of morbidity and mortality. Burma has a National Strategic Plan for 2010 – 2015 that sets malaria control goals to achieve the Millennium Development Goals.

Approximately 62% of the population of the country lives in malaria risk areas (21.4% in high risk, 17.9% in moderate risk and 22.4% in low risk areas). The malaria burden in Burma is estimated by WHO to be 1.5 million (range: 1.35 – 1.66 million), Malaria morbidity (per 1,000 populations) and mortality (per 100,000 populations) came down sharply from 24.4and 12.6 in 1990 to 11.2 and 1.2 respectively in 2011.*Plasmodium falciparum* and *P. vivax* are the major species of malaria parasite, with the occasional reports of *P. malariae* and *P. ovale. Plasmodium falciparum* accounts for 70-80% of cases with a slight decline in occurrence of *P. falciparum* over the past decade.

Forest-related workers, miners, seasonal migrant workers/farmers, pregnant women and children under five years of age are the risk groups. According to the malaria data base in 2011, adult males accounted for 65% of total blood-confirmed cases, reflecting the risk attributed to occupations such as mining, forest-related activities, construction, rubber tapping, etc. While the number of malaria deaths has fallen in the past decade, the number of reported cases has not. These data need to be interpreted with caution, however, as the number of cases confirmed by microscopy and especially RDTs has increased tremendously. Furthermore, reported data represent only the public sector and are thought to reflect only 25-40% of the total burden. In 2011, the public sector and non-governmental organizations (NGOs) working under the Global Fund Round 9 grant reported 617,540 combined outpatient and inpatient malaria cases.

Areas of concern for artemisinin resistance have been identified within Burma through ongoing drug resistance monitoring. In 2009-2010, the early signs of *P. falciparum* resistance to artemisinins characterized by prolonged parasite clearance time were reported in at least three States/Regions (Mon, Tanintharyi and Bago-East); and evidence of suspected artemisinin resistance was reported in Kachin, Kayah and Kayin States. As an emergency response, a strategic framework to contain the resistance strains was developed and endorsed in 2011. The Myanmar Artemisinin Resistance Containment Project(MARC) activities were started in mid-2011.

Malaria control in Burma is led by National Malaria Control Program (NMCP) and is implemented by the Vector Borne Diseases Control (VBDC) program, Department of Health, Ministry of Health with the collaboration of partners from public and private sectors. At central level, the VBDC program is mandated to formulate national strategies, policies, standards and norms related to malaria control, provide training, conduct operational research (OR), control of outbreaks, and provide consultative and advisory services to implementing agencies.

The Malaria Technical and Strategy Group (TSG) under the leadership of VBDC and with technical assistance from WHO comprises technical experts from the Ministry of Health (MOH), United Nations agencies, national and international NGOs, and donors, including PMI. Within this group, a core group comprising VBDC, United Nations Children's Fund, Japan International Cooperation Agency, selected NGOs and WHO held periodic meetings for improved coordination. It serves as a forum for technical matters and, as necessary, provides inputs to the Myanmar Country Coordination Mechanism.

A key challenge faced by the VBDC in Burma has been a lack of resources. Burma ranks among the lowest countries in the world in per capita health expenditures, and, while the program promotes sound, comprehensive approaches to malaria control, it lacks sufficient resources to implement those plans. Following termination of the Global Fund Round 3 support, the Three Diseases Fund [a multi-donor trust fund consisting of European Commission, UK Department for International Development (DFID), AusAID, and the governments of Norway, the Netherlands, and Sweden] was established in August 2006. The Three Diseases Fund has contributed approximately $4 million per year over the past several years to malaria control, allowing the program to successfully implement case management and preventive programs in limited areas. After the ending of the Three Diseases Fund, the seven-donor consortium contributed to a new Three Millennium Development Goal Fund that included some investments in malaria.

With the Global Fund Round 9 grant, Burma's NMCP expanded access to parasitological diagnosis and treatment with ACTs. The program works at the community level through a network of village health volunteers who carry out either preventive measures only (e.g., BCC, mass treatment of mosquito nets, and distribution of LLINs) or prevention measures and case management in villages where access to health facilities is very difficult. The scope of work will be expanded further with Global Fund New Funding Mechanism and Regional Initiative on Artemisinin Resistance Containment.

These additional resources will allow the program to continue to protect at-risk populations with ITNs/LLINs. The program's objective is to ensure that 80% of the population in moderate- to high-risk areas is protected with ITNs/LLINs. The use of IRS was halted in the early 1990s; however, the program continues to promote its selected use in situations, such as outbreaks or new development projects.

Cambodia

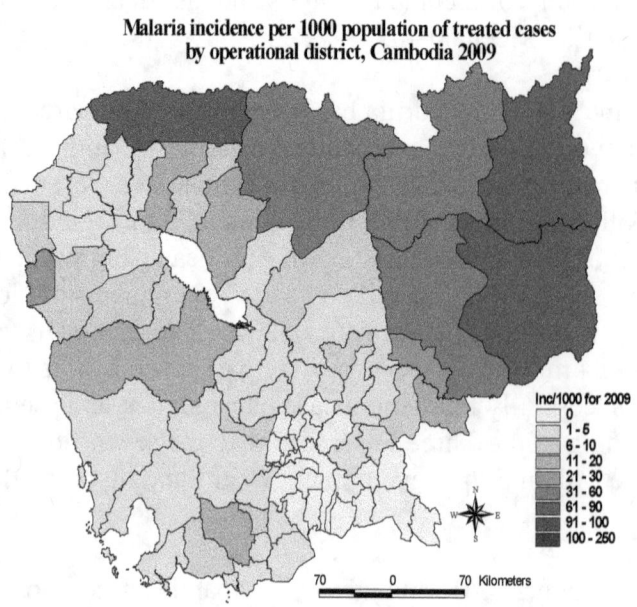

Malaria incidence per 1000 population of treated cases by operational district, Cambodia 2009

Inc/1000 for 2009
- 0
- 1 - 5
- 6 - 10
- 11 - 20
- 21 - 30
- 31 - 60
- 61 - 90
- 91 - 100
- 100 - 250

70   0   70 Kilometers

Decades of civil war, including the genocide and systematic destruction of infrastructure under the Khmer Rouge regime left Cambodia with a limited health infrastructure, particularly in rural areas; however, over the last decade, many of Cambodia's key health indicators have improved as the country's economy has developed. Malaria nevertheless remains a major contributor to the public health and economic burden in Cambodia, with a reported incidence in the public sector of 4.3 cases per 1,000 population in 2011. Various surveys have reported 67-80% of sick persons (68% in the 2010 Cambodia Malaria Indicator Survey) seeking treatment in the private sector; thus at least 300,000 to 400,000 new cases of malaria could be treated in the private and informal sector annually. Eighty percent of the population lives in areas without malaria transmission, but around 20% (approximately 2.9 million people) either live permanently in the forested endemic areas or are "forest dependent" for additional income. The 2010 Cambodia National Malaria Survey estimated a malaria prevalence of 0.9% in high-risk areas (<2km from the forest), a reduction from the 2.9% reported in 2007. Transmission is seasonal, in the forest and forest-fringe areas of the north, west and northeast, and also in the rubber plantations of the east and northeast. Development of cassava, corn and fruit orchards has contributed to favorable conditions for local malaria vectors where migrant workers are common. In the rice growing areas of the south and central regions, transmission is low or non-existent. There is no transmission in urban areas. Low intensity transmission is found locally in coastal areas. According to the health management information system (HMIS), confirmed malaria is predominantly observed in males aged 15-49 years (51%). Both malaria morbidity and mortality rates have declined over the last decade due to an increased government commitment together with substantial additional financial and technical support from the international community.

The National Centre for Parasitology, Entomology, and Malaria, formally referred to as the National Malaria Centre (CNM), sits within the MOH. The leadership of the malaria control activities within Cambodia rests at the central level; however, with the decentralization of the MOH, Provincial Health Department and Operational District malaria supervisors are involved with planning and implementing activities. Participation of Village Malaria Workers (VMWs),

Village Health Volunteers (VHVs), Mobile Malaria Workers (MMWs) and local authorities helps improve the availability and accessibility of malaria services, including early diagnosis and treatment, LLIN distribution, and malaria health education.

The national case management policy in Cambodia is to ensure access to quality diagnosis and treatment of positive cases with the ACT, dihydroartemisinin-piperaquine (DHA-Pip), which has been made available countrywide in public health facilities and through trained VMWs. ACTs are used to treat both falciparum and vivax malaria. In response to the reduced efficacy of DHA-Pip, newly revised national treatment guidelines authorize the use of Malarone in Pailin (Zone 1); the use of single-dose primaquine to block transmission of falciparum malaria has been temporarily put on hold in the absence of safety data or a point-of-careglucose-6-phosphate dehydrogenase (G6PD) test. Malarone is provided as directly observed therapy. The burden of malaria among mobile, migrant, and cross-border populations remains high and presents a huge challenge for prevention and control. Monotherapies may still be found in the unregulated private sector in Cambodia, despite efforts to ensure availability of high quality antimalarials. With the increased resources associated with successful Global Fund grants, overall ITN ownership improved from 43% in high-risk areas in 2007[3] to 75% in 2010[4]. Cambodia has drafted a new strategic plan following the Prime Minister's announcement that Cambodia will seek to eliminate malaria by 2025.

Following so far unreleased findings of deficiencies in Global Fund programs, the United Nations Office for Project Services (UNOPS) has become the Principal Recipient of Global Fund funds with CNM designated as "Principal Implementing Partner." Continuing grants are awaiting signatures; however, additional changes may occur during 2013. Effects on field programs have been minimal so far. WHO has recently established its regional hub for Emergency Response to Artemisinin Resistance, based in Phnom Penh; this activity, while regional in nature, may bring increased technical support to Cambodia.

---

[3] Cambodia National Malaria Survey, 2007
[4] Cambodia National Malaria Survey, 2010

Thailand

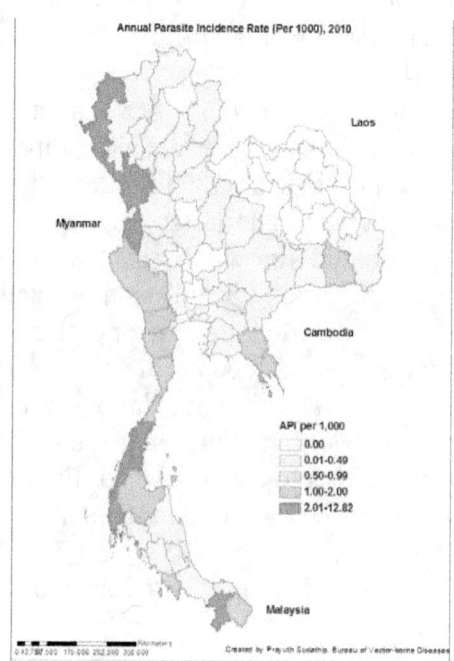

Malaria cases mainly occur in the border provinces, especially near the Burmese border. The groups at risk for malaria in Thailand consist of migrants, mobile populations, refugees in camps, those spending nights in the forest; ethnic minority groups are particularly affected. In 2009, Thailand reported a higher number of cases among foreigners than Thai nationals. Between 2001 and 2010, Thailand has noted a drop in the number of cases from 63,528 to 32,480 and deaths from 848 to 80.

The Thai NMCP is located within the Bureau of Vector-Borne Diseases (BVBD), Department of Disease Control, within the Ministry of Public Health (MOPH). The program operates vertically in areas where malaria transmission still occurs; in areas where indigenous transmission has been eliminated it provides only technical assistance and programmatic responsibilities have been transferred to Provincial Public Health Offices. The National Strategic Plan for Malaria Control and Elimination 2011–2020 seeks to free 80% of the country from malaria transmission by the year 2020.

The country has done an excellent job of extending diagnostic services to endemic areas through malaria clinics and posts. The staff in these facilities use either microscopy or RDTs. Patients testing positive for falciparum malaria are treated with mefloquine and artesunate per national policy and with Malarone in selected zones of the artemisinin resistance containment project. In both these settings, a single dose of primaquine is provided for gametocytocidal effect without prior G6PD testing.

With Global Fund Round 10 support, the BVBD will continue containment activities and expand their focus beyond the Thai-Cambodian border to include the Thai-Burma border. Round 10 support will increase LLIN coverage to 100% (approximately two persons per LLIN) amongst Thai citizens and long-term, non-Thai residents. In addition, LLINs for short-term, non-Thai residents will be provided when the person presents at a clinic with fever. Long-lasting insecticide-treated hammock nets (LLIHNs) and repellents will also be provided to special at-risk populations. In the event of a documented local focus of infection, the NMCP plans to conduct limited IRS in the areas near the index cases.

Other important components of the Thai national strategy include a comprehensive approach to migrant and mobile populations, enhanced BCC activities, OR, and intensified surveillance and monitoring &evaluation (M&E). *In-vivo* antimalarial drug efficacy studies have identified additional sites in Thailand with an increased proportion of day three positive blood smears and increased ACT failure rates at day 28. These sites include Ranong, Kanchanaburi, Tak, and Mae Hong Son, all located along the border with Burma.

China

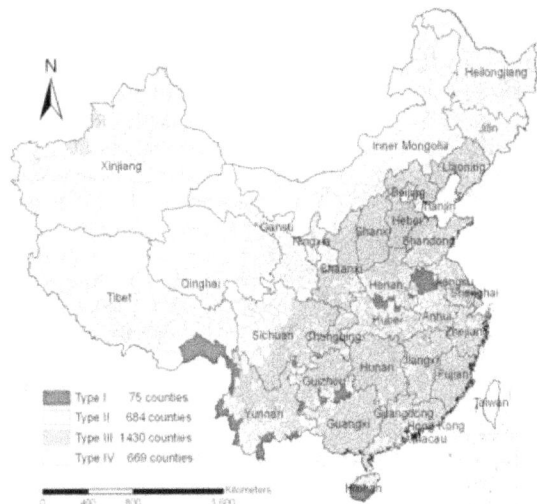

The People's Republic of China is mainly affected by *P. vivax; P. falciparum* is endemic in only two provinces, Yunnan and Hainan. Because Yunnan Province shares borders with Burma, Laos, and Vietnam, it is the province in China of greatest concern for malaria and, as such, is included in regional GMS malaria control strategies. The Bureau of Disease Control located within the MOH is responsible for managing malaria control activities while the Provincial Health and County Health Bureaus manage the provincial- and county-level efforts. The new 2010–2020 National Malaria Strategy aims to eliminate malaria from all provinces by 2020 with an intermediate goal of elimination from all areas except the borders of Yunnan Province by 2015.[5] In China, counties are classified by type (e.g. Type I counties have an incidence of >1/10,000, Type II counties have an incidence <1/10,000, Type III counties have no local cases for three years, and Type IV are malaria free). In Yunnan, Type I counties are concentrated along the Burma border where malaria is particularly problematic among people crossing the border and ethnic minority groups. Although China has demonstrated a decline in malaria

---

[5] From Malaria Control to Elimination: A Revised National Malaria Strategy 2010-2015. The People's Republic of China

morbidity and mortality, control efforts are hampered by the continuous influx of migrants from Burma.

The Chinese treatment policy calls for use of ACTs, primarily DHA-Pip. The strategy for vector control is based on epidemiologic stratification. In the high risk areas with vector presence, the program aims to achieve 100% LLIN coverage and to use indoor residual spraying (IRS) in focal transmission areas. Additionally, the program designs specific interventions for special populations such as forest workers and migrant populations.

Lao PDR

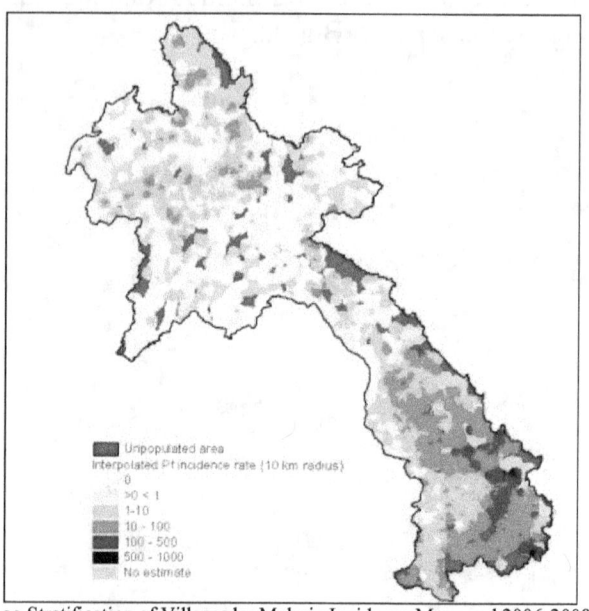

Lao Stratification of Villages by Malaria Incidence Measured 2006-2008

The intensity of malaria transmission varies between different ecological zones: from very low transmission in the plains along the Mekong River and in areas of high altitude, to intense transmission in remote, hilly and forested areas. *Plasmodium falciparum* is the predominant species, accounting for 95% of all recorded malaria cases, although recent surveys suggest a *P. vivax* prevalence rate of around 25%. Transmission is perennial but with large seasonal and regional variations. Groups at greatest risk include ethnic minorities, forest and agricultural workers, miners, and children below the age of five years. Significant reductions in malaria transmission have been reported since the large-scale introduction of ACTs and ITNs, in conjunction with socioeconomic and environmental changes. The annual number of uncomplicated malaria cases (probable and confirmed) fell from 40,106 in 2000 to 20,800 cases in 2010 and the number of malaria deaths in hospitals dropped from 350 in 2000 to 24 in 2010; however, the influx of seasonal workers of mainly Vietnamese origin has led to alarming increases of reported malaria cases in southern and eastern provinces bordering Vietnam.

Beginning in 2011, Centre for Malaria, Parasitology, and Entomology (CMPE) began utilizing a more targeted approach to the distribution of malaria control measures. As detailed in their 2011-2015 National Strategy for Malaria Control and Pre-Elimination, rather than providing ITNs, RDTs, and ACTs in all villages, these resources were to be reserved for the villages with the highest burden of malaria[i]. A survey of all malaria cases reported between 2006-2008 in each village was performed in 2009, and villages were stratified based on malaria incidence into four groups: Stratum 1 (0-0.1 cases/1000 persons), Stratum 2 (0.1-10 cases/1000 persons), Stratum 3 (>10 cases/10000 persons) and Unknown (insufficient data). About two-thirds of the villages were determined to fall into Stratum 1, and the rest were divided between the remaining strata. Most of the low-strata villages were in the north, whereas high-strata villages tended to be concentrated in the south.

According to the National Strategy, only Strata 2 and 3 villages received routine ITN distribution. Village health workers in strata 3 continued to receive RDTs, ACTs, and a small stipend to perform educational activities. Village health volunteers in Strata 1 and Unknown risk villages were encouraged to perform educational activities, but did not receive additional resources. Routine operational activities under the National Strategy were largely funded through the Global Fund, whereas most salary support was provided by the Lao PDR Government. Malaria control measures were further decreased in 2010 when a delay in the receipt of funding and supplies led to a lack of LLIN distribution, even in high-incidence strata.

In November 2011, CMPE was notified about increasing malaria cases being reported in Attapeu Province in the southeast corner of Laos. CMPE quickly responded by increasing supplies of RDTs and ACTs to the area. A locally active NGO, Health Poverty Action secured funding from the European Commission Humanitarian Organization for a more comprehensive outbreak response from January-June, 2012. This included the mobilization of LLINs, RDTs, and ACTs to the affected villages. In addition, active case detection, mobile clinics, and tri-lingual BCC materials were used to try to reach high-risk populations.

The Department of Disease Control, CMPE, WHO, and Health Poverty Action all contributed to an investigation of the outbreak. In their reports, they concluded that the outbreak was related to increased mobilization of workers to the area for employment, a lapse in bed net distribution in 2010, and a prolonged rainy season in 2011[ii,iii]. They noted specific concern about cross-country and cross-border migration of workers, a lack of health planning for employees of large dam construction and rubber plantation companies, and increased forest activities including illegal logging for foreign companies or individuals. While much of this information was obtained through key informant interviews, a review of the epidemiological data from the province confirmed that most of the malaria cases were occurring in men over 15 years of age, consistent with a likely employment-related exposure. Following a presentation of these findings, PMI contributed nearly 30,000 LLINs, 7,000 long-lasting insecticide treated hammock nets and 40,000 ACT treatments to aide in the outbreak response in Attapeu.

Vietnam

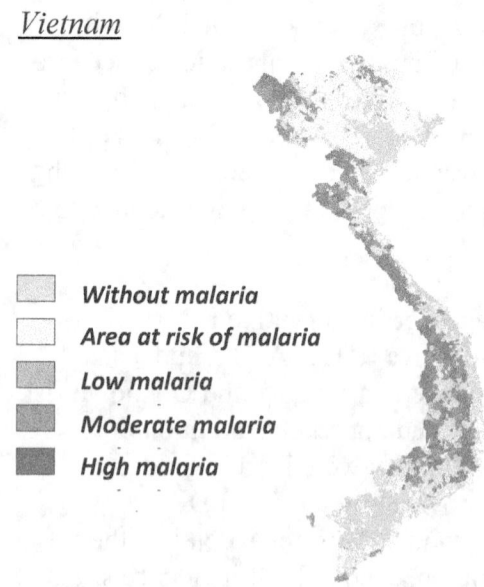

Without malaria
Area at risk of malaria
Low malaria
Moderate malaria
High malaria

2009

Malaria occurs in remote forest and forest fringe communities, which are often inhabited by marginalized groups, including ethnic minorities and migrant settlers. The distribution of ITNs has occurred in all endemic villages with a coverage estimated to be 70% by the NMCP. The program retreats approximately 4 to 5 million bednets each year. In addition to this, the NMCP uses IRS to cover an additional two million people residing in hyper-endemic areas, where ITNs use is low. The burden is concentrated at the border areas of Cambodia and Lao PDR. Vietnam has reduced malaria cases and deaths from 274,910 to 54,297 and from 142 to 21, respectively, between 2000 and 2010.

The National Institute for Malariology, Parasitology, and Entomology (NIMPE) rests within the Ministry of Health. Since the government changed strategies from eradication to control in the early 1990s, it began to prioritize interventions toward case management, prevention (ITNs and IRS), and health education. The NIMPE recently drafted a National Strategy for Malaria Control, Prevention and Elimination in Vietnam through 2020 with the goals of continuing to roll back malaria in meso-and hyper-endemic areas and implementing a step-by-step malaria elimination strategy in the low endemic areas, which has been endorsed by the prime minister.

CURRENT STATUS OF MALARIA INDICATORS

Although some of the standard indicators adopted in the GMS differ from those in Africa, several indicators, mostly measuring net ownership and use, remain applicable to this sub-region. The following table shows the most recent figures for the standard indicators being used by PMI, where survey data are available:

Table 3. National and sub-national survey data for the GMS countries

Indicator	Burma (MARC 2011-2012)	Cambodia (CMS 2010)	Cambodia (Migrants Zone 1, 2010-2011)	Thailand (Global Fund 2009)	Thailand (Migrant, Ranong 2012)	Lao PDR (Bednet 2009)	Vietnam (MICS 2006)
Malaria prevalence (%)	0.5	0.9	-	-	0	-	-
Households with at least one net (%)	97.4	99.4	-	-	83-94	-	99
Households with at least one ITN (%)	35.1	74.7	25-53	-	-	90	19
Persons who slept under an ITN the previous night (%)	15.9	52.6	6-27	36	1-2	-	-
Children under five years old who slept under an ITN the previous night (%)	19.4	56.3	-	-	-	81	5
Pregnant women who slept under an ITN the previous night (%)	20.3	59.1	-	-	-	-	-
MARC: Myanmar Artemisinin Resistance Containment Project; CMS: Cambodia Malaria Survey; ITN: insecticide-treated net; MCC: Malaria Control in Cambodia; MICS: Multi-Indicator Cluster Survey; R7: Global Fund to Fight AIDS, Tuberculosis and Malaria Round 7							

Most of the GMS countries have relied primarily on routine HMIS data for planning and monitoring their malaria activities, but more recent evaluation plans include cross-sectional, representative surveys. The exception has been Cambodia, which has conducted national malaria surveys in 2004, 2007, and in 2010, as well as a Demographic and Health Survey (DHS) in 2010. Burma conducted a survey in containment zones 1 and 2 that sampled households, health facilities, and drug outlets in late 2011 as part of the MARC Project. Other countries with national intervention coverage, but not prevalence data include Lao PDR where a national bednet survey was conducted in 2009 and Vietnam with a Multiple Indicator Cluster Survey in 2006. Overall, these surveys from the sub-region show high levels of conventional bednet ownership with low levels of ITN ownership and use, with the exception of Lao PDR. Malaria prevalence estimates from both Cambodia and Burma show very low levels at <1%; however, Burma was sampled after the peak transmission season. Migrant surveys using respondent driven sampling methodology to generate a representative estimates show lower levels of ITN ownership and use compared to the resident populations both in Cambodia at the Thai border and in Thailand at the southern Burmese border. Thailand completed a national household survey with Global Fund support in late 2012 and the results are pending. Similarly, Lao PDR completed a DHS with a malaria module in 2011-12 showing relatively high ITN coverage, but lower use of appropriate diagnostics and treatment.. Lastly, Cambodia plans to conduct a follow-up national survey in 2013 and there are ongoing discussions regarding a national Malaria Indicator Survey (MIS) in Burma.

Routine program, surveillance and survey data for relevant PMI indicators are shown in Table 4. The Control and Prevention (CAP)-Malaria Project has been gathering baseline info from the three focus countries. They are currently in the process of gathering baseline data for Thailand. In Cambodia, their baseline data are a combination of the final results from their previous Malaria Control in Cambodia Project for six operational districts and new survey results from their three new districts, while Burma data are derived from two surveys conducted in 2012. Preliminary baseline survey results are included in Table 4 from Burma and Cambodia.

Table 4. CAP-Malaria project areas

Indicators	Burma (Kawthaung, Tanintharyi)	Burma (Kayin)*	Cambodia (6 MCC ODs)	Cambodia (3 new ODs)
Household survey data	**2012**	**2012**	**2011**	**2012-2013**
Households with at least one net (%)		87.9	97	99.7
Households with at least one ITN (%)		37.8	45	
Net use the previous night (%)	92.1	42.9	84	96.8
ITN use the previous night (%)	68.7			81
*preliminary; ITN- insecticide-treated nets				

Indicators	Burma	Cambodia	Thailand
Target population (FY 2012)	1,598,018	2,200,000	1,448,000
Target population (FY 2014)	3,824,239	3,008,317	1,448,000
Malaria cases	79,000	13,239	
Programmatic data (October 2011– December 2012)			
LLINs/LLIHNs distributed	39,800	1,071,056	None
Health education: no. of people reached	34,543	298,113	9,783
Malaria cases tested	14,855	107,476	2040 (61% non-Thai)
Malaria cases treated	1,924	25,539	63 (55% non-Thai)
Test positivity rate (%)	13	24	3
No of people trained on diagnosis / ACT treatment	536	259	442 (21 migrant volunteers)
Entomology surveillance	4 sites	2 sites	2 sites
Percentage of cases with parasites detected on day 3 after treatment with an ACT (WHO TES)	5-10% (AL); 13-20% (DHA-Pip); 27% (AS)		0-14% (A+M)
Percentage of cases with parasites detected on day 3 after treatment with an ACT (community Day 3 surveillance)		0-10.5%	31% (A+M)
ACT- artemisinin-based combination therapy; LLIN- long-lasting insecticide-treated nets; LLIHN- long-lasting insecticide-treated hammock nets			

CURRENT FUNDING SITUATION

The tremendous progress made in the region to date has paralleled the increase in malaria funding from external sources. As a whole, the region has been very successful in obtaining support from the Global Fund. All six countries have had at least one Global Fund grant totalingover$500 million for the GMS as a whole. The table below details the various recent Global Fund grants from the six countries. It also includes domestic funding where the data was available and additional major funding sources in the sub-region, e.g. Three Diseases Fund and BMGF. This table includes current and active funding, and does not include potential future funding. Global Fund proposals have been submitted by Burma, Thailand, Cambodia, Lao PDR and Vietnam and are in various stages of review in 2013. Burma is an early applicant to the Global Fund Transitional Funding Mechanism and five countries will submit proposals for the Global Fund's Regional Artemisinin Resistance Initiative announced in March 2013.

Table 5. Current funding in the GMS

Country	Funding	Total Budget in USD (Funds Disbursed)	Activities
Regional	AusAID	5,000,000	WHO regional Emergency Response for Artemisinin Resistance Project
	BMGF	10,000,000	
	BMGF	7,500,000	Therapeutic Efficacy Surveillance network
	BMGF	3,000,000	Drug treatment operational research
Burma	Domestic*	1,259,002	Staff salaries, trainings, limited quantity of drugs and diagnostics, IEC materials, reporting forms, infrastructure and operational costs.
	Three Diseases Fund	25,500,000	National response to malaria control and implementation of MARC framework. Support provided in 26 townships (Tiers 1& 2).
	BMGF and DFID	24,000,000 (8,000,000)	Replacement of artemisinin monotherapy in the private sector.
	Global Fund R9	35,298,428 (33,129,349)	Prevention, case management and capacity building of health care providers in 226 townships.
Cambodia	Domestic*	3,127,120	Treatment services for Cambodian citizens (2012 Funding)
	Global Fund R9	50,953,325	Pre-elimination (April 2013 – June 2015)
	Clinton Health Access Init.	<100,000	Technical assistance for procurement and supply management and public-private partnerships.
China	Domestic*		None reported in WMR 2012
	Global Fund R6	12,312,206 (11,865,704)	Focus on Chinese migrant workers and local residents on the Myanmar border and cross-border collaboration
	Global Fund	79,476,904 (61,483,848)	Elimination
	Global Fund R10	5,080,078 (3,223,364)	Intensified malaria control along the Myanmar-China border. Implementing only the 2-year Phase 1 (January 2012-December 2013).

	Domestic*	1,040,000	Treatment services for Lao citizens
Lao PDR	Global Fund Transitional Funding Mechanism	6,440,000	LLIN scale-up activities, early diagnosis and treatment, Information System, project management; private sector involvement in five southern provinces (July 2013 – June 2015).
Thailand	Domestic*	509,577	Treatment services for Thai citizens (2012 Funding)
	Global Fund R7	17,515,927 (15,526,805)	Focus on migrants and communities in conflict zones
	Global Fund	29,203,469 (16,347,131)	Containment of artemisinin resistance and moving towards the elimination of plasmodium falciparum
Vietnam	Domestic*	4,545,455	Treatment services for Vietnamese citizens
	Global FundR7	24,780,695 (19,968,595)	Community-based targeting the remaining endemic areas and mobile populations
	BMGF	187,000	Malaria Drug Resistance
Source: World Malaria Report 2012, www.theglobalfund.org, www.gatesfoundation.org, www.Three Diseases Fund.org; Figures in parentheses are disbursed amounts; *Funding per year			

GOAL AND TARGETS OF THE PRESIDENT'S MALARIA INITIATIVE IN THE GMS

In line with the Lantos-Hyde Malaria Strategy[6], PMI will work with NMCPs and partners to strengthen the response to multidrug resistant *Plasmodium falciparum* malaria in the GMS. The USG strategy states that this will be accomplished by:
- Supporting well-functioning antimalarial drug resistance surveillance networks in each country in the region;
- Establishing national systems to monitor the quality of antimalarial drugs as a means of preventing the introduction and dissemination of sub-standard or counterfeit drugs, which contribute to increased drug resistance; and
- Contributing to a further reduction in the level of transmission of *P. falciparum* malaria and the number of reported cases in the Greater Sub-Mekong Region.

For PMI GMS, the goal of limiting the spread of multidrug resistant malaria will be accomplished through three programmatic sub-objectives guiding the FY 2014 MOP activities and their implementation at regional and country levels. The three sub-objectives are:
1. To strengthen malaria prevention and control interventions in focus areas with existing or emerging artemisinin resistant malaria.
2. To ensure effective drug efficacy surveillance networks to monitor artemisinin resistant malaria throughout the GMS.
3. To monitor the quality of antimalarial drugs throughout the GMS and build country capacity to prevent the availability of sub-standard or counterfeit drugs.

---

[6]Lantos-Hyde USG Malaria Strategy 2009–2014

At a regional level, the PMI GMS activities will support efforts to conduct therapeutic efficacy studies to monitor artemisinin resistance in all six countries and with particular intensity in areas where there is evidence of confirmed or potential emergence of artemisinin resistance. PMI will lead this effort and ensure technical capacity and timely reporting with engagement of national governments to take ownership of these efforts and encourage cost-sharing as other interested donors provide resources for expansion. PMI will also support efforts to monitor drug quality, ensure that critical bottlenecks in the supply chain system are removed to ensure availability of the most effective antimalarials, address impediments to the availability of effective commodities, and combat use of sub-standard and counterfeit drugs that contribute to increased drug resistance.

The FY 2014 MOP activities focus on areas of documented and threatened artemisinin resistance in Burma, Cambodia and Thailand, specifically:

- Tanintharyi Division and Kayin and Rakhine States in Burma
- Fourteen operational districts along Cambodia's borders with Thailand, Lao PDR and Vietnam
- Tak, Kanchanaburi, Ranong, Trat and Chanthaburi and possibly other provinces in Thailand threatened by artemisinin resistance.

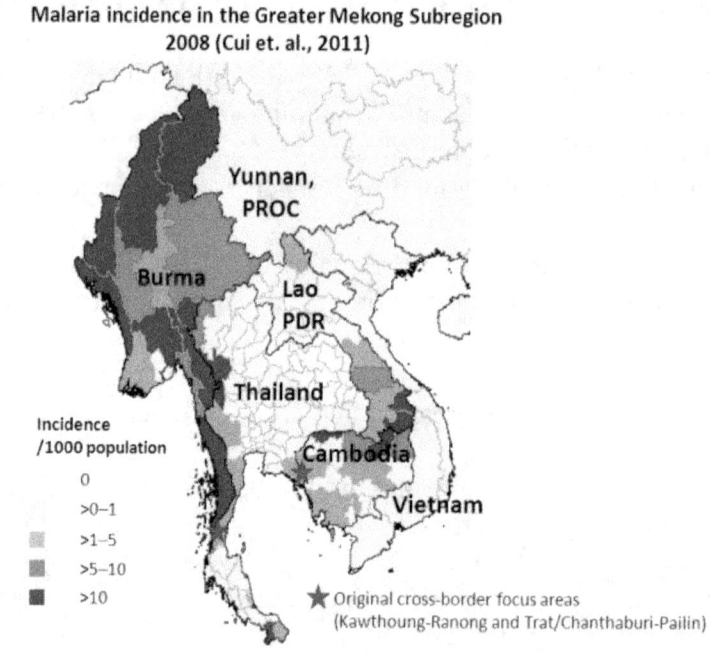

Malaria incidence in the Greater Mekong Subregion 2008 (Cui et. al., 2011)

To support the goals and objectives of the PMI GMS, the following indicators are proposed:

1) To strengthen malaria prevention and control measures in focus areas with existing or threatened artemisinin-resistant malaria:
   - Confirmed malaria cases (number and rate) (target: 50% decrease by 2015 compared to 2010)

- In-patient deaths due to malaria (number and rate) (target: 50% decrease by 2015 compared to 2010)
- Percentage of households at risk of malaria that own at least one ITN (target: 100% by 2015)
- Percentage of individuals in areas at risk of malaria who slept under an ITN the previous night (target: 90% by 2015)

2) To ensure effective drug efficacy surveillance networks to monitor artemisinin-resistant malaria throughout the GMS:
- Number of PMI-supported sites completing drug efficacy studies (target: 35 sites over 2 years)

3) To monitor the quality of antimalarial drugs throughout the GMS and build country capacity to prevent the availability of sub-standard or counterfeit drugs:
- Percentage of drugs identified during post-market surveillance to be substandard or counterfeit (target: <5% by 2015)

EXPECTED RESULTS — YEAR FOUR

By the end of Year 4 of PMI in the GMS, the following targets under the three programmatic objectives will have been met:

1. To strengthen malaria prevention and control measures in focus areas with existing or threatened artemisinin-resistant malaria.

   Focal malaria control areas

   Prevention:
   - In Year 4, approximately 506,000 LLINs/LLIHNs will be procured and distributed free of charge in the PMI cross-border focus areas to protect targeted vulnerable and high-risk mobile and migrant populations through various community-based distribution mechanisms.

   Treatment:
   - RDTs (approximately 1,050,000) and ACTs (approximately 300,000) will be procured to fill any gaps in the cross-border focus areas.
   - Approximately 1,500 community malaria volunteers (700 in Cambodia and 800in Burma) in the targeted focus areas will provide malaria prevention and control services to targeted populations including migrant and mobile groups.

   M&E:
   - Surveillance systems strengthened and baseline routine surveillance and survey data collected for the malaria control focus areas.

2. To ensure effective drug efficacy surveillance networks to monitor artemisinin-resistant malaria throughout the GMS

   Regional— GMS 6 countries

   Drug Efficacy Surveillance:

- Over 17 out of 35 PMI-supported sites across six countries in the regional network will have conducted therapeutic efficacy studies (testing conducted at each site every two years).

3. To monitor the quality of antimalarial drugs throughout the GMS and build country capacity to prevent the availability of sub-standard or counterfeit drugs:

Regional— GMS 6 countries
Drug Quality:
- Antimalarial drugs sampled for quality in Thailand, Burma and Cambodia and strengthening of host country systems in drug monitoring, policy and enforcement.

PREVENTION ACTIVITIES

Insecticide-Treated Mosquito Nets and Indoor Residual Spraying

All NMCPs in the GMS support the mass free distribution of LLINs to targeted areas, especially where there is suspected artemisinin resistance. In addition to LLINs, there is provision – sometimes at no cost and sometimes through social marketing – of long lasting insecticide-treated hammock nets (LLIHNs), intended for forest workers. Traditionally, there has been a very large and active private sector sale of untreated nets of varying quality throughout the GMS. Household ownership of untreated nets is high, especially in rural Burma and Cambodia; thus, both of these NMCPs include net retreatment with a long-lasting insecticide as part of their strategies.

At least 10 of the 36 species of anopheline mosquitoes recognized in the GMS are involved in malaria transmission. Primary vectors are *An. dirus*, *An. minimus* and/or *An. maculatus*; however, vector status and relative importance can change with location and season. Several other species are considered secondary vectors which usually play minor roles in transmission, but which can assume greater roles with changes in ecology and human/animal behavior. An example of this occurred in 1974, when after a cyclone in the Rakhine State of Burma reduced the cattle population and *An. sundaicus* (*epiroticus*) changed its feeding habits from cattle to humans resulting in a major malaria outbreak.

Much of the malaria transmission in the GMS occurs in forested and forest fringe areas, plantations and farms where workers sleep in the open or under temporary shelters. Some reports indicate that up to 60% of infective bites occur either outdoors, or during the evening or early morning hours when people are not sleeping. The consensus of 2012 and 2013 meetings of the Roll Back Malaria Vector Control Working Group on outdoor malaria transmission was that LLINs/LLIHNs are effective in the GMS and wide coverage of vulnerable populations should remain a goal, with high priority given for the development and evaluation of methods to interrupt outdoor transmission. In a summary of ten publications on the efficacy of ITNs in South East Asia, eight studies reported broad effectiveness; one study reported effectiveness against one vector species but not others, and one found no measurable effectiveness against any host mosquitoes. (Efficacy of insecticide treated nets in South East Asia: Annotated Bibliography by Anna Hoskin, Malaria Consortium report, Sept 2010).

Mosquito coils, repellents, protective clothing and fumigation with smoke are also used within the GMS as personal protective measures. A presentation at the 2013 Vector Control Working Group meeting reported that most rubber tappers in Burma used mosquito coils attached to a hat or head lamp when tapping. There have been several efforts in Burma, Thailand, Cambodia and Vietnam to reinforce personal protection through use of repellents and treated materials; however, the use and effectiveness of topical repellents in different settings has not been assessed and widespread deployment has not occurred. Preliminary results of a large-scale repellent study in Cambodia showed no added protection with repellent use. There is an urgent need to identify and test new, efficacious personal protection measures for vulnerable groups.

While IRS appears in strategy documents for the GMS countries, it is now rarely used, being difficult to efficiently target and implement. Implementation of IRS in Thailand, as in Burma and Cambodia, is limited. All three countries state that they will implement IRS in "outbreak" areas or where there is active transmission. At the present time, PMI will not fund IRS implementation in any GMS country.

Burma
According to the 2010-2015 National Strategic Plan for Malaria Control, Burma's VBDC Program aims to achieve 80% coverage of the population in moderate and high-risk areas using ITNs and LLINs by 2015. The NMCP strategy classifies a total of 284 townships as endemic, of which 180 are targeted for scaling up coverage of LLINs/ITNs and retreatment of nets. The strategy has an objective of two LLINs/ITNs per household, provided free, through mass distribution campaigns to the population of 15.5 million residing in high and moderate risk areas within the 180 townships, with replacement of the LLIN after three or five years, depending on the type of net though durability studies have not been conducted.

As with other countries in the region, there is a high rate of conventional net use. According to the 2010–2015 National Strategic Plan for Malaria Control, many families in Burma already use mosquito nets, but rates are highly variable and many nets are untreated. A 2008 survey by the Myanmar Council of Churches conducted in 160 malaria endemic and hard-to-reach villages in Chin State, Kachin State and Sagaing Division showed that 91% of households own any type of mosquito net (treated and untreated) with an average of two nets per household. However, coverage of nets treated with insecticide (e.g., ITNs or LLINs) is very low, with only an estimated 5.6% of the total population protected by any ITN. Similarly, in the more recent MARC survey, household ownership of nets was 97%, but ITN and LLIN ownership only 35% and 18%, respectively.

The Burma VBDC recognizes the importance of the private sector and the need for a clear policy articulating its role. According to a recent LLIN assessment report[7] (May 2012), a vibrant retail market exists with several untreated cotton net brands available in a variety of colors. Consumers prefer longer, softer opaque fabric nets that are used for privacy. In addition to imported nets from China, Thailand and Vietnam, the Burmese government produces and supplies conventional nets through special government supply shops known as "Win Thuza."

---

[7] Networks Project: Vector Control Assessment in Greater Mekong Sub-region and Review of Malaria Prevention Strategies (Draft May 2012)

The LLIN retail market is in its early stages with only PermaNet® available for sale in Burma; the majority of WHOPES-approved LLIN brands are not registered and must be before entering the market.

Burma's LLIN needs are met primarily through the Global Fund Round 9 grant which covers 14 of the 17 states and divisions and a population estimated to be approximately 40.9 million in 2008. Most of the targeted townships are in the eastern and southern part of the country where treatment failures and prolonged parasite clearance time for ACTs have been reported. In 2011 and 2012, 1.3 million LLINs were distributed and 2.5 million conventional nets retreated using all sources of support, including the Global Fund. The Three Millennium Development Goal Fund is also expected to contribute approximately 900,000 LLINs in 2013 but exact quantities are unknown at this time. Due to the inaccessibility of certain areas in Burma, there will most likely be LLIN gaps. With the cancellation of the Global Fund Round 11, funding gaps for LLINs and malaria commodities are anticipated in Burma. PMI will focus its efforts on filling gaps in LLIN procurement and distribution in the cross-border focus areas.

Cambodia
Cambodia has a strong "net culture". The national malaria survey from 2010 indicated that 99% of households owned at least one mosquito net; however, just 75% had an ITN, and only 53% of all respondents reported sleeping under an ITN the previous night. The proportion who slept under an ITN the previous night was 56% for children under five years and 59% for pregnant women.

Cambodia's 2011-2015 National Strategic Plan for Elimination of Malaria calls for universal access to preventive measures among target populations, including mosquito control, personal protection and environmental manipulation, together with community awareness and behavior change among the population at risk. The strategy calls for one LLIN per person and one LLIHN per family provided for free to those living in villages at risk as well as the retreatment of existing conventional nets with long-lasting insecticide. Nearly three million people, living less than 2 km from the forest edge, are targeted for LLINs and hammock nets. Mobile and migrant populations will receive one LLIN distributed either free or on loan from large-scale employers. Under the Global Fund Rounds 6 and 9 grants, the CNM has distributed 3,642,000 LLINs between 2011 and 2012. There are no plans for additional procurements in 2013. Approximately 350,000 LLINs are planned for 2014 from all resources to be distributed through campaigns. The national program faces challenges with transporting nets from the operational districts to the health centers, as well as maintaining adequate stocks and storage facilities.

Cambodia has a large number of privately-purchased untreated nets, and it is estimated that 900,000 untreated nets are imported every year. Unlike programs in Africa, partners' support has been provided for a net treatment scheme for untreated nets in Cambodia. Supported by Global Fund Round 9, Population Services International (PSI) implemented a 'bundling strategy' to ensure that a long-lasting insecticide retreatment kit (ICON MAXX®) was bundled along with 70% of all commercially available family-size and hammock nets *before* the nets were released onto the market; this activity ended recently. Most of the estimated 900,000 untreated nets imported and sold in Cambodia each year are moderately priced, affordable, and attractive, coming in an array of colors and styles, making these nets extremely appealing to the Cambodian consumer. In 2011 and 2012, an estimated 700,000 retreatment kits were targeted for distribution in the private sector. The average price of a bundled net to a consumer ranges from $2.50 to $5.00, which under the 'bundling strategy' included a free retreatment kit.

Thailand

The Thai BVBD's National Strategic Plan for Malaria Control and Elimination targets one LLIN per each resident, long-term migrant, and military personnel based in malaria endemic villages. LLINs are to be replaced every three years. Long-lasting insecticide hammock nets are distributed in endemic villages of targeted provinces where LLINs cannot be used (e.g., migrants and soldiers spending nights in the forest and on the Thai-Cambodia border). Thailand is a major net manufacturer.

Good estimates of untreated net coverage in Thailand are not available. Use is thought to be lower than in neighboring areas of Burma and Cambodia, but this may also be due to the better construction of housing in Thailand. According to data presented during the Thailand Malaria Program Review in August 2011, of the 2.1 million persons at risk in Thailand, 780,858 were protected by IRS and 1.8 million were protected by ITNs/LLINs in 2010.

Under Thailand's Global Fund Round 10 grant, 600,000 LLINs were distributed free-of-charge in mass campaigns between October 2011 and March 2013 in 22 endemic target districts. Further efforts are needed to increase access to LLINs for hard-to-reach populations, especially mobile and migrant populations. PMI will fill commodity gaps and provide targeted support for migrants in the focus cross-border areas in Trat/Chanthaburi, Kanchanaburi, Ranong, Tak and possibly other areas along the border where artemisinin resistance may be a problem.

Historically, IRS with DDT has been shown to be effective against *An. minimus* in northern Thailand. Approximately 160,000 structures are sprayed annually (deltamethrin, 2 rounds/year). Other vector control measures include space spraying targeting infected mosquitos to control outbreaks; repellents for persons with outdoor activities at night; environmental management (cleaning vegetation on stream edges); and larvivorous fish.

Progress to Date:

With FY 2011 funds, PMI assessed policies, strategies, and gaps in funding and distribution of ITNs in targeted GMS countries (particularly on Burma, Cambodia and Thailand). PMI is using the findings to further assist countries in refining their programmatic and operational ITN strategies. Regional gap analyses have changed rapidly because of major changes in Global Fund financing as well as significant but temporary procurement delays. PMI will work with NMCPs and implementing partners over the next year to gather information on LLIN gaps and needs.

To help address urgent needs and protect vulnerable populations, with FY 2011 funding, PMI procured and distributed approximately 230,000 LLINs in focal areas in Burma. With FY 2012 funds, PMI will procure 145,000 LLINs for Burma, Lao PDR, and Cambodia to fill gaps. With FY 2012 funds, 110,000 LLINs were provided to Thailand to cover migrants in 26 provinces, with the majority distributed in Tak Province bordering Burma and Chanthaburi and Srakeo Provinces bordering Cambodia. With FY 2013 funds, PMI will procure approximately 325,000 for free distribution in the PMI cross-border focus areas to protect targeted vulnerable and high-risk mobile and migrant populations through various community-based distribution mechanisms.

Planned activities with FY 2014 funding are as follows: ($2,655,000 total: $1,575,000 Burma, $730,000 Cambodia, $350,000 Regional)

- **Procurement and distribution of LLINs and LLIHNs:** Although the GMS countries have funding from the Global Fund to cover most needs, PMI will procure approximately 506,000 LLINs and hammock nets for the GMS region to fill LLIN gaps at the household level in villages and townships in the cross-border focus areas and those that are not supported under the current Global Fund agreement, including reaching migrant and mobile populations with LLINs. PMI estimates LLINs based on prior year's consumption and the quantities distributed by implementing partners who are working with marginalized populations mainly through workplace and outreach distribution channels. PMI will reserve a limited quantity of LLINs and LLIHNs to respond to emergency needs in the region.
    a. **Burma:** PMI will procure 300,000 LLINs for focus areas to fill gaps and reach high risk vulnerable populations including migrants and mobile populations. ($1,125,000)
    b. **Cambodia:** PMI will procure and deliver 100,000 LLINs and hammock nets in 14 focus operational districts in Cambodia, filling potential gaps and targeting migrant and mobile populations. ($350,000)
    c. **Regional:** PMI will support procurement of 86,000 LLINs and LLIHNs for focus areas in Thailand and to fill potential gaps in the region. ($300,000)

- **Community-level support for distribution, promotion and use of ITNs:** PMI will support distribution and delivery of LLINs through mass distribution to reach households, BCC to promote use of LLINs and treated material/hammock nets. PMI will primarily target the cross-border focus areas in Burma and Cambodia with possible geographic extension along the border areas, depending on the existing gaps and PMI resources. Some support will also be provided to ensure cross-border reach in Thailand, particularly focused in the border areas of Ranong, Trat/ Chantaburi, and possibly Tak and Kanchanaburi Provinces. In Cambodia and Thailand, special efforts will be made to reach cross-border migrant populations and other vulnerable groups (forest, plantation, and farm workers).
    a. **Burma:** PMI will distribute LLINs to households as well as vulnerable populations living and working in focus areas and promote their use through trained village malaria volunteers. ($450,000)
    b. **Cambodia:** PMI will distribute LLINs and LLIHNs to employers of seasonal migrant workers and to residents at the household level in specific targeted districts and promote their use. ($280,000)
    c. **Regional:** PMI will support distribution costs for LLINs and LLIHNs and promote its use in focus areas of Thailand. ($50,000)

- **Net User Preference assessment:** PMI will support efforts in Cambodia to assess current net use and preferences to guide LLIN procurement and retreatment policy. Since a large number of untreated nets are privately-purchased in the GMS, PMI will identify barriers to LLIN use by targeted households and understand preferences that are appealing to consumers and associated with procurement decisions of commercially available nets to include: price, size, style (round/rectangular/hammock), denier (unit of fineness), privacy, color, insecticide treatment, etc. There is evidence in Cambodia from a number of sources to indicate that

34

people have a strong preference for untreated cotton nets. Although some studies have touched upon net preferences, the information from these studies has been limited to date. The proposed PMI assessment would conduct focus groups with target populations to obtain more in-depth information and inform strategies to enhance LLIN use.

a. **Cambodia:** Assessment to identify user preferences in nets and hammocks. ($100,000)

Malaria in Pregnancy

Within the GMS PMI supports a two-pronged approach to reduce the burden of malaria infection among pregnant women including provision of LLINs and effective case management of malaria and anemia, especially amongst the most vulnerable populations including migrant workers, refugees, and other hard-to-reach populations. IPTp is not part of any national strategy in the GMS. NMCP strategies support distribution of LLINs to households in areas of confirmed artemisinin-resistance but there are no national policies for provision of nets to pregnant women attending antenatal care (ANC) services. The percentage of households with at least one ITN in Cambodia is approximately 75% (2010) while in Burma household coverage of an ITN is 35% (2011-12). LLIN use among pregnant women ranges from 60% (2010) in Cambodia to 20% (2011-12) in Burma.

National malaria treatment policies for pregnant women follow WHO recommendations: quinine is used in the first trimester and ACTs in the second and third trimesters. ANC attendance is generally high in all GMS countries: most pregnant women attend ANC at least once (89% of women in Cambodia, 99% in Thailand and 80% in Burma) and most pregnant women complete the recommended four visits (80% of women in Thailand, 73% in Burma); however only 27% of pregnant women attend a fourth ANC visit in Cambodia.

Control of malaria in pregnancy and implementation of strategies in the Mekong Sub-region are complicated by heterogeneous transmission settings, coexistence of multidrug resistant *P. falciparum* and *P. vivax* parasites and different vectors. A review of malaria in pregnancy in the Asia-Pacific region[8] (2012) reported that recommendations on regimens to use in treatment of malaria during pregnancy are absent in many settings, and in practice, health workers may not be prescribing antimalarials correctly or are reluctant to give drugs to pregnant women because of potential harmful effects. The report identified a disconnect between routine antenatal practices and recommended prevention and treatment policies for malaria in pregnancy.

Burma
Data on the burden of malaria in pregnancy in the region is limited. A 2002 review in Burma reported a low prevalence of clinically suspected malaria among pregnant women (1-2% of total outpatient and inpatient burden). A separate 2005 study found that 11% of pregnant women attending antenatal care and 12% of all women delivering in Eastern Shan State and Mon State were infected with malaria. The states and divisions identified with the highest incidence are Rakhine, Kachin and Kayah. Wide variations in prevalence of malaria parasitemia in women attending antenatal care services were reported, ranging from 3% in Tanintharyi Division to 37%

---

[8] Malaria in pregnancy in the Asia-Pacific region: Marcus J Riken et al; Lancet 2012 (12: 75-88).

elsewhere along the Thai-Burma border, where the majority of women were asymptomatic and infected with *P. falciparum.* Women's role as migrants may also be underestimated in the region; small studies conducted by PMI partners in Burma found more than 50% of migrants in their catchment areas are women.

Cambodia
Cambodia undertook a study in Ratanakiri Province with the highest malaria burden in order to assess malaria in pregnancy. With USAID funding, WHO supported the Ratanakiri Provincial Health Department to implement a malaria screening strategy (or intermittent screening and treatment) for pregnant women using RDTs as part of antenatal care in three selected health centers. Results showed a malaria prevalence of 5% at health centers and 6% at the village level. Screening for malaria is introduced in the treatment guidelines, but the NMCP has not yet implemented such as strategy.

Regional
Research from Thailand has indicated that even when the point prevalence of malaria infection in pregnant women is very low (e.g. less than 1%), cumulative prevalence over the term of the pregnancy may be as high as 36% (Shoklo Malaria Research Unit).

Progress to Date:
With FY 2011 funds, PMI supported a rapid assessment of malaria in pregnancy to identify programmatic areas that needed strengthening. The assessment found limited information on the burden of malaria in pregnancy and a lack of coordination between maternal child health and malaria control departments within ministries of health. The role of pregnant women as carriers of resistant parasites both as residents and migrants and the management of drug-resistant malaria in pregnant women have not been addressed in the region. Other major hurdles included limited training available for maternal child health staff and midwives on malaria in pregnancy and lack of integrated policies, guidelines or training materials for health staff supporting maternal child health, reproductive health and disease control programs. The report recommends collecting accurate data on the burden of malaria in pregnancy; adapting policies and practices to the rapidly changing epidemiological situations; and developing focused ANC strategies that emphasize care and management of malaria in pregnancy especially when ANC takes place in different epidemiological settings. Access to care for pregnant women in remote and mobile populations remains a challenge in all countries in the region, with the risk of malaria infection in pregnancy highest in areas that are least accessible. Countries also need to develop ethnically appropriate BCC materials and messages directed to the prevention and early treatment-seeking for suspected malaria. With FY 2013 funding, PMI will begin to address these recommendations by assisting ministries to revise policies especially for areas of confirmed artemisinin resistance, ensuring integration of malaria in pregnancy across relevant national programs and improving data on pregnant malaria patients at all health system levels.

Planned activities with FY 2014 funding are as follows: ($100,000 Total: $50,000 Burma, $50,000 Cambodia)

- **Strengthen malaria in pregnancy and focused ANC practices:** Based on the recent assessment and activities initiated with FY 2013 funding, PMI will continue to support malaria in pregnancy activities in Burma and Cambodia by updating guidelines, training and supervision materials and ensuring consistency across maternal health and malaria programs.

a. **Burma:** PMI will support regular coordination meetings between malaria and maternal health programs to review data and refine policies. PMI will support the development of ethnically appropriate BCC materials for the prevention and early treatment-seeking of malaria among pregnant women and for use by village malaria volunteers and midwives. ($50,000)

b. **Cambodia:** PMI will continue to ensure close coordination of policies, treatment guidelines and regimens, and training materials and BCC messages on malaria in pregnancy across the Maternal Child Health Program and the CNM. PMI will work with CNM to review and possibly address challenges with implementing intermittent screening and treatment. PMI will develop local language BCC messages and produce materials for low-literacy audiences. PMI will continue to review training and supervision materials used by maternal child health staff and midwifery schools in coordination with the CNM. ($50,000)

CASE MANAGEMENT

Malaria Diagnosis

National malaria diagnosis policies in all GMS countries require confirmatory testing with either microscopy or an RDT before treatment for malaria can be prescribed. In hospitals and higher-level health facilities, microscopy is the preferred diagnostic method. RDTs now have been scaled-up in lower level facilities and through VMWs, MMWs, and Village Health Workers (VHWs). With support of the Global Fund and other partners, RDTs also have been scaled-up in Cambodia and have been introduced through a social franchising approach provided to clinics and village volunteers in Burma. Because both *P. falciparum* and *P. vivax* are present throughout the GMS, national programs promote RDTs that can detect both species.

Burma

The status of the Government of Burma's reported 700 malaria microscopy centers remains unclear, although only about 60% are reported to be functioning adequately. A quality assurance system was initiated in 2005, with training and technical support provided by WHO and ACT Malaria, but the quality of diagnostic testing is unknown.

Microscopy is the preferred diagnostic method, but its availability is limited primarily to townships. In addition, the majority of persons with malaria seek treatment from private sector providers, where diagnostic testing may not be available or may be of poor quality. Even in health facilities that do have malaria microscopy, some health providers continue to treat patients for malaria based on clinical signs and symptoms alone.

VHWs have been trained to diagnose malaria with RDTs and provide treatment with ACTs, but only in a limited number of townships in the Thai-Burma border area, although progress has been made on expanding the number of villages with VHWs.

In the private sector, the Population Services International (PSI) "Sun Quality Network" Project operates a private sector franchise of clinics and shops which has now scaled-up to 874 Sun Quality Health Clinics in 206 townships. These clinics provide an array of services, including diagnosis of malaria with RDTs and treatment of confirmed cases with ACTs. In addition, 1,507 VHWs have also been trained in malaria diagnosis and treatment through the Sun Quality Primary Care network. Through this Sun Quality Network, approximately 400,000 RDTs have been performed and 100,000 ACTs have been prescribed.

Cambodia

Almost all public sector facilities in Cambodia have the capacity to conduct confirmatory testing for malaria, in most cases using microscopy. Almost all suspected malaria cases are confirmed by diagnostic testing in these facilities. VMWs and MMWs, who have been trained to perform RDTs and treat confirmed malaria cases with ACTs, also have been deployed in most villages in the Zone 1 containment areas of Western Cambodia, with some limited expansion into Zone 2.

An end-of-project assessment of USAID's Malaria Control in Cambodia Project found that none of the 971 patients diagnosed at health facility or community level in the project target area with suspected malaria were treated without first having a diagnostic test. PMI's support has been essential to maintain the success of this program, including key support for routine supervision, quality assurance, and refresher training activities, plus implementation of a community supply system linked to the existing health facility system, close monitoring of diagnostic stock levels at operational division warehouses, reinforcing and strengthening logistic management at peripheral level, and maintenance of buffer stocks of laboratory commodities. Outside of these targeted areas, the quality of malaria diagnosis is of variable quality, particularly in remote health facilities. When RDTs are available, health workers prefer using RDTs over microscopy, because of their ease of use.

As in Burma, many Cambodians often prefer to access care in the private sector. With Global Fund support, a network of private sector providers, in small clinics and drug shops, has been trained and provided with subsidized RDTs and ACTs. Use of RDTs in these outlets has increased significantly since their introduction, but progress has been hampered by a few nationwide stock-outs. Despite this challenge, adherence to the RDT results has improved, with two-thirds of those with negative tests not being prescribed ACTs.

Thailand

In high transmission areas, a network of 280 malaria clinics with malaria microscopy and 394 malaria posts using RDTs has been established. The BVBD conducts quality assurance monitoring for microscopy. Active case detection using microscopy and/or RDTs is carried out in high-risk villages and towns and in the artemisinin resistance containment zones. BVBD, in collaboration with Provincial Health Offices, also is targeting hard-to-reach populations in high-risk border areas through the development of special service facilities where RDTs are available. Some NGOs provide primary health care services, including malaria case management, to 140,000 refugees along the Thai-Burma border.

Progress to Date:

Burma

With FY 2012 funding, PMI procured 238,500 RDTs. To date, 536 VHWs have been trained in malaria case management, including diagnostic testing, in focus townships in Tanintharyi and Kayin. These VHWs have performed 14,855 RDTs on patients with suspected malaria and treated 1,924 of those with ACTs.

Cambodia

In the last year, 24,000 RDTs and 25 microscopes were procured with FY 2012 funding. PMI continued supervision and supportive activities to 481 VMWs, including training/re-training of 259 VMWs. Quality assurance activities were carried out in targeted laboratories in Western Cambodia. Through these VMWs, 107,476 patients were tested for malaria, of which 25,539 patients were treated for malaria with ACTs.

Thailand/Regional

Training was provided to 448 health workers and volunteers in Thailand, including 21 migrant volunteers. As a result of PMI support activities, 2,040 suspected malaria cases received a diagnostic test, of which 61% were migrants from other countries. Sixty-three were diagnosed with malaria and treated; half of these were non-Thai migrants.

PMI also supported a regional workshop on quality assurance of malaria microscopy, which was attended by representatives of all countries in the GMS. Refresher training also was provided to 13 national-level trainers from Burma, Thailand, and Cambodia. Four trainers from these three countries also underwent the WHO accreditation training, with eight of the participants achieving a Level 1 or Level 2 certification (i.e., expert level).

Planned activities with FY 2014 funding: ($1,430,000Total: $800,000 Burma, $500,000 Cambodia, $130,000 Regional)

PMI will continue support for diagnostic testing at facility and community level in Cambodia and Thailand and scale-up diagnostic testing at community level and primary care level in Burma through the provision of commodities, refresher training of existing laboratory staff and health workers in the performance and use of malaria microscopy and RDTs, and strengthening quality assurance systems. Specifically, PMI will:

- **Procure RDTs and microscopy supplies.** PMI will procure multi-species RDTs and reagents and supplies for microscopy to fill gaps in country requirements, particularly for migrant and mobile populations. This will include:
    a. **Burma:** approximately 600,000 RDTs primarily for VHWs in target townships in Tanintharyi Division and Kayin and Rakhine States. ($400,000)
    b. **Cambodia:** approximately 300,000 RDTs and microscopy supplies for target operational districts. ($200,000)
    c. **Regional:** approximately 150,000 RDTs and microscopy supplies to fill unanticipated gaps in countries in the GMS. ($50,000)

- **Training, supervision, and quality assurance of RDTs and microscopy.** Additional VMWs/VHWs will be trained in malaria case management, including the performance of RDTs in PMI focus areas of Burma and Cambodia. Refresher training also will be provided to existing VMWs/ VHWs, and health facility clinicians and laboratory staff. (Costs included in treatment section)

- **Support strengthening national diagnostics quality assurance/quality control (QA/QC) system:** PMI will provide technical assistance and training of key staff to strengthen the national reference laboratory. Activities will include a baseline assessment to determine current activities and gaps. Based on the baseline assessment, support could include training of laboratory staff, updating of national diagnostic policies, and support for development of tools and standard operating procedures.
    a. **Burma:** strengthening national diagnostics QA/QC system. ($100,000)

- **Private sector quality assurance:** The Global Fund currently provides support for commodities, training, and supervision to 874 private sector clinicians and 1507 VHWs in Burma through the Sun Quality Network. The Global Fund also provides commodities, training and medical detailing to approximately 1,800 private sector clinics and drug shops in Cambodia.
    a. **Burma:** PMI will provide support for the expansion of the Sun Quality Network into additional high-risk areas for malaria in Burma, with a focus on quality assurance of case management services.($300,000)
    b. **Cambodia:** PMI also will provide targeted support to improve quality assurance activities through routine supervision and also to develop and implement a reporting system to capture case information, which will be incorporated into the Cambodian national malaria surveillance system.($300,000)

- **Training and accreditation for microscopy:** PMI will continue support for the training and accreditation of supervisors of malaria microscopy throughout the GMS. This training is essential for maintenance of a cadre of expert laboratory technicians who will in turn supervise and train front-line health workers.
    a. **Regional:** support for microscopy training and accreditation. ($80,000)

Malaria Treatment

All GMS countries have enhanced their case management activities in response to the increasing problem of artemisinin resistance, particularly to assure that parasitological diagnoses are obtained prior to administering treatment for uncomplicated cases. Because of the possibility that resistance may lead to clinical failure, several GMS treatment guidelines call for patients to be followed up at regular intervals to ensure cure.

Patients presenting to clinics in areas of suspected resistance now undergo more rigorous follow-up to monitor the response to therapy, including routine collection of a blood smear on the third day (D3) after initiation of treatment to determine the proportion of patients with persistent parasitemia. Determination of sites with a high proportion of D3 positive cases, a possible harbinger of artemisinin resistance, is particularly important for the region, since the goal of limiting the spread of multidrug resistant malaria will be accomplished through drug efficacy surveillance networks to monitor artemisinin-resistant clones. Although this has traditionally been accomplished via standard *in vivo* therapeutic efficacy studies (TES), D3 monitoring may be crucial important in areas where traditional TES monitoring may not be feasible. National Malaria Control Programs and PMI continue to work together where D3 surveillance is employed to develop appropriate response measures.

Village Malaria Workers serve as a community focal point at the sub-district level for prompt diagnosis, BCC messaging, and provision of appropriate and timely treatment and often receive training and support from the nearest sub-district level malaria clinic or post. Countries continue to employ VMWs for diagnosis and treatment services in less accessible areas. With implementation of D3 surveillance, the role of VMWs has expanded in the realm of surveillance and continued follow up to document that slow-clearing parasites are eventually cured.

In Thailand, Cambodia and Laos, health facility workers generally receive regular supervision and refresher training under the technical leadership of their NMCPs. Such training opportunities may not be offered to all health care providers; however, PMI will continue to fill training gaps concentrating on quality case management at the community level.

The role played by the private sector in providing malaria treatments varies greatly throughout the region. Thailand banned the sale of antimalarials in the private sector in 1995, and ACTs are almost never seen in private outlets. In contrast, private sector sales account for the majority of malaria treatments provided in Cambodia and probably also in Burma. The Global Fund and other donors have supported activities in both Cambodia and Burma for improving access to quality ACTs in the private sector. In Cambodia, a social marketing program provides diagnosis and subsidized, high-quality ACTs. In Burma, a network of social franchises (Sun Quality Health and Sun Primary Health) provides similar services. In Burma, a new subsidized ACT treatment project has been launched in the retail private sector that has been successful in removing artemisinin monotherapy from many retail outlets.

Progress to Date:
PMI continues to maintain a flexible approach to fill gaps for treatments at facility and community level in Cambodia and Thailand and at the community level and primary care level in Burma. Activities are largely concentrated in border areas where transmission and concern for artemisinin resistance tend to be highest.

Burma
In 2012, PMI established 14 new fixed and mobile malaria clinics, training workers on WHO and NMCP protocols for malaria treatment. PMI supplied 68,070 ACT treatments to established border malaria posts in townships along the border with Thailand. Each mobile team covers approximately 30 zones or villages within the township and each village is visited by a mobile health team at least monthly.

Cambodia

PMI continues to provide training community-level workers on diagnosis and treatment, emphasizing delivering care to migrants, largely through VMWs and MMWs. In 2013PMI funding was used to recruit 80 new VMWs and provide training to 118 village and facility based health workers.

Thailand

Case management activities in Thailand are concentrated mainly in Trat/Chanthaburi, Tak and Ranong Provinces along the border areas. PMI supported 33 malaria posts and clinics in Ranong and Tak Provinces, providing training for 201 health care workers in case management, and in Trat and Chanthaburi Provinces, services were provided by mobile malaria clinics in eight sub-districts. In 2012, control of 18 border malaria posts transitioned to the MOH in a pilot program to support integration of malaria care into the public sector.

Planned activities with FY 2014 funding ($4,060,000 Total: $2,150,000 Burma, $1,600,000 Cambodia, $310,000 Regional)

Throughout the GMS, requirements for ACTs continue to be met largely by the Global Fund, national governments, and other donors. The PMI will continue to fill critical gaps when supply chain or financial lapses impede ACT availability. For treatment-related case management activities, training and supervision must be sustained in the target areas and conducted in expanded geographic areas where providers may not be familiar with best practices. Technical support for supervision of case management also is required in Thailand, particularly in light of the introduction of a new treatment regimen. PMI will support the following activities:

- **Procure ACTs:** PMI will procure approximately 300,000 ACT treatments across the GMS.
    a. **Burma:** approximately 150,000 ACT treatments primarily for VHWs in target townships in PMI target areas. ($150,000)
    b. **Cambodia:** approximately 100,000 ACT treatments for use by community-level volunteers targeting migrant or mobile populations in 14 target operational districts. ($100,000)
    c. **Regional:** approximately 50,000 ACT treatments to fill unanticipated or emergency commodity gaps in GMS countries. ($50,000)

- **Training and supervision of diagnostics and case management at facility and community levels in PMI focus areas:** Support will be provided to train and supervise VMWs and malaria post/clinic staff focusing on adherence to various NMCP treatment guidelines and delivery of malaria prevention and control services to high risk populations.
    a. **Burma:** Training and supervision in diagnostics and case management for VHWs in all 580 targeted villages (approximately 680 persons trained, assuming attrition of 100 VHWs) and approximately 120 rural health center staff, and strengthening capacity of state- and township-level health management teams to support facility and community services. ($2,000,000)
    b. **Cambodia:** Training and supervision of 700 VMWs in 14 ODs, implement active case detection activities, and refresher training in support of NMCP policies. ($1,500,000)

c. **Regional:** Training and supervision at malaria treatment facilities and community workers in PMI focus areas.($120,000)

- **Operational support at malaria posts and clinics:**
  a. **Thailand**: Support for training and supervision of clinical and laboratory staff at33malaria posts/clinics (18 in Ranong and 15 in Mae Sot) supervised by BVBD. Training will focus on case management in areas with high-risk populations in Trat/Chanthaburi and Ranong Provinces, but may be expanded to other areas at the Thai-Burma border.($140,000)

Pharmaceutical management

Effective malaria case management requires that efficacious, high-quality antimalarials are available and used by both providers and patients according to national guidelines. Even with high-quality drugs, incomplete or inappropriate treatment can lead to failures requiring additional treatment, as well as contributing to selection of resistant parasite strains. Ensuring the availability and use of antimalarial medicines, diagnostics and preventive commodities is a high priority for PMI.

Burma
Health commodities are procured and distributed in Burma in two ways: through the VBDC; and the CMSD. The VBDC distributes laboratory supplies and antimalarial drugs to township hospitals and health departments throughout Burma. Additionally, it supplies sub-national VBDC teams located in states and divisions. Township health departments then are responsible for the distribution to the station hospitals, rural health centers, and sub-rural health centers. The second system managed by the CMSD is within the Medical Care Services of the Department of Health. The CMSD purchases antimalarial drugs using government funds in consultation with the VBDC. CMSD distributes to all township hospitals and health departments. Since 2002, UNICEF has supported Supply System Management Officers whose duty it is to strengthen the supply and logistics systems within the Ministry of Health.

The private sector is a key source of care in Burma. The PSI Sun Quality Health project operates a private sector franchise of clinics and shops. The procurement of commodities and logistics for this network of private sector clinics is carried out by PSI with Global Fund Round 9 support.

Global Fund Round 9 funding covers ACTs, RDTs and other malaria medicines for 240 of the 284 malaria endemic townships. VBDC will provide the services in all 240 townships with support from other partners. Procurement for ACTs and other malaria medicines is handled by the two Primary Recipients - Save the Children and United Nations Office for Project Services (UNOPS) - for their sub-recipients. The Global Fund proposal assumes that 879,000 cases of malaria will be treated with ACTs in 2012 and 754,000 in 2013. The proposal also estimates that approximately 1.1 million fevers will be tested with RDTs in 2012.The Three Millennium Development Goals Fund (formerly The Three Diseases Fund) imports malaria commodities on behalf of implementing partners, including WHO/NMCP.

PMI support for pharmaceutical management and commodities to Burma primarily consists of monitoring availability of commodities (medicines, diagnostics, and nets) supplied through the Global Fund; facilitating procurement and distribution of PMI-funded commodities to fill gaps not addressed by the Global Fund grant; and providing targeted technical assistance, micro-planning, and/or logistics support as needed to support full coverage of malaria interventions in the focus areas of Tanintharyi Division and Kayin and Rakhine States. Special attention will be paid to support community-level logistics to target cross-border migrants through the development of simple inventory tools, storage and transport boxes, etc.

Cambodia
In Cambodia, approximately 67% to 80% of fever patients are estimated to seek care in the private sector, in part because the public health system is weak and not easily accessible and commodity stock-outs have been a major problem. Last year, Cambodia transitioned its first-line treatment for malaria from artesunate-mefloquine to DHA-Pip for both *P. falciparum* and *P. vivax*.

The Central Medical Stores (CMS) is responsible for the procurement and logistics of essential medicines to the public sector. The CMS operates an integrated logistics system that procures and distributes medicines to the operational district stores and national hospitals every quarter. The operational district stores are supposed to make requests for essential medicines including antimalarial drugs to the CMS. Medicines are provided free-of-charge to the districts, but user fees at service delivery sites vary by facility and are often a barrier to seeking diagnostic and treatment services by the poor. The CMS operates an integrated logistics management information system. The NMCP has developed a web portal into this system to better monitor the movement and availability of malaria pharmaceutical products in the CMS system.

Cambodia has long been involved with the private sector. In an effort to improve the quality of antimalarials sold by these providers, PSI/Cambodia embarked upon a pilot project in 2002 exploring the possibilities of a socially-marketed ACT named Malarine (artesunate plus mefloquine). The pilot was successful, and PSI scaled up the program which distributes WHO-pre-qualified ACTs and RDTs to private clinics, pharmacies, and shops throughout rural Cambodia. Populations Services International manages all aspects of the in-country supply chain; thus, stock-outs are limited to procurement delays at the national level. Supplies of ACTs and RDTs for both the public and private sector in Cambodia are provided through the Global Fund Round 9 funds.

As in Burma, PMI is supporting strengthening the supply chain management to facilitate procurement and distribution of PMI-funded commodities; and provide targeted technical assistance, micro-planning, and/or logistics support as needed to ensure full coverage of malaria interventions, particularly in the target operational districts along the Thai, Lao, and Vietnamese borders. Special attention will be paid to community-level logistics to target cross-border migrants through the development of simple inventory tools, storage and transport boxes, etc.

Thailand
In order to achieve the goal of early diagnosis and treatment of malaria cases in Thailand, the NMCP manages the delivery of commodities to facilities, particularly to the public sector

malaria clinics and posts. Although a USAID-supported assessment in Thailand revealed that there are some challenges in the pharmaceutical management and supply system, overall capacity and performance is strong. When there are problems with stock availability, drugs are exchanged between facilities and districts.

The recent Thai Malaria Program Review found that logistics and pharmaceutical management systems in the border provinces, particularly reaching migrant and mobile populations, need improvement. The review also recommended consideration of a stockpile for medicines and diagnostics for potential epidemics. PMI support for pharmaceutical management in Thailand will primarily focus on these priorities and micro-logistics for migrant and mobile populations in the targeted focus areas of Ranong and Trat/ Chanthaburi Provinces.

Regional

The PMI will provide limited pharmaceutical management support to the other countries in the region, as requested. The challenges and limitations are common to most pharmaceutical management logistic systems including delays in reporting, completeness and the collection of data. PMI plans to initiate support for, and implementation of, a procurement planning and monitoring report for malaria in targeted GMS countries which will report product availability at central levels to serve as an early warning system to avoid stockouts, providing another means for on-going monitoring of commodity availability and system performance.

A regional proposal for the Global Fund is under development and will include Thailand, Laos, Burma, Vietnam, and Cambodia. It is anticipated that the grant will include country specific and regional activities.

Progress to Date:

PMI is providing support to strengthen pharmaceutical management and supply chain systems in the region through the procurement of supplies and strengthening the in-country systems that manage them. Activities are organized around improving system performance and visibility to ensure that malaria products are available when and where they are needed, strengthening in-country supply systems and enhancing the capacity for effective management of malaria commodity supply chain. The PMI has supported an assessment in the region of national counterpart abilities to provide supply chain monitoring data and has also supported the placing of a resident logistics advisor based in Phnom Penh, Cambodia to provide technical assistance toward the compiling, analyzing and dissemination of supply chain information.

The PMI has begun to monitor regional malaria commodity pipelines so potential bottlenecks in procurement and distribution of malaria commodities (including Global Fund financed commodities) can be quickly addressed and availability of key commodities ensured. A preliminary assessment of quantification processes in some GMS countries has contributed to a better understanding the NMCP's capabilities to monitoring commodities, resources, and gaps. The regionally-based technical advisor is providing information on malaria commodity pipelines for the region, analyzing potential gaps and weaknesses, as well as supporting various supply chain management activities on behalf of partners.

Planned activities with FY 2014 funding ($300,000 total: $150,000 Burma, $100,000 Cambodia, $50,000 Regional)

- **Support for pharmaceutical management and logistics:** PMI will monitor and address potential bottlenecks in procurement and distribution of malaria commodities (including Global Fund-financed commodities) to ensure availability of key commodities in focal areas as well as to respond to urgent requests. Key priorities for each country are listed above. Support will be provided to all GMS countries, as needed, particularly to assist on commodity issues with respect to Global Fund grant implementation.
    a. **Burma**: Support for strengthening supply chain management and logistic systems. ($150,000)
    b. **Cambodia**: Support for strengthening supply chain management to ensure the availability of key commodities in targeted focal areas. ($100,000)
    c. **Regional**: Support for strengthening supply chain management systems in the region. ($50,000)

Drug Quality

The USG has a strong commitment in the GMS to improve the quality of antimalarial drugs. Over the past decade, USAID has supported the establishment of a regional approach to monitoring drug quality by training key staff within national programs and medicine regulatory agencies to travel into the field and periodically test randomly collected antimalarials for quality. The presence of counterfeit drugs with no active ingredient can result in the patient going untreated and possibly dying. Substandard drugs, including those with less than an appropriate amount of active ingredients, lead to sub-therapeutic blood levels and may contribute to the development of drug resistance. Other key challenges include inadequate quality assurance/quality control of medicines, weak regulatory enforcement, manufacturers not compliant with good manufacturing practices, availability of artemisinin monotherapy, and the presence of multiple brands of antimalarial drugs on the market that are hard to regulate.

The USG, through United States Pharmacopeia (USP) has established a regional program of 54 sentinel sites throughout the GMS that periodically monitor antimalarial drugs. Through dynamic sampling, USP collects samples from geographic areas around each site to prevent counterfeiters from being able to make sales to specific vendors or villages without being detected. In addition, USP provides capacity building support to national quality control laboratories and has initiated a Network of Official Medicines Control Laboratories to enable south-to-south cooperation and to foster the exchange of expertise between national drug quality leaders from around the region. This new initiative is designed, in part, as catalyst to enhance the operation of the Asian Network of Excellence in Quality Assurance of Medicines, which was established in late 2006 to promote expertise and skills in Good Manufacturing Practices and quality control through training and workshops.

Burma
Given the large quantities and varieties of antimalarials available in the private sector, the high number of malaria cases in the country, and the country's relative poverty, Burma is felt to be

vulnerable to the introduction and sale of counterfeit and substandard antimalarial drugs and artemisinin monotherapies. There have even been anecdotal reports of counterfeits in Burma resulting in patients dying. In 2009, WHO/USP found that most of the staff who had been trained to conduct drug quality testing were no longer present, nor were there adequate equipment and reagents. In addition, the national reference laboratory at the Food and Drug Administration (FDA) has only one high performance liquid chromatography machine and one refurbished dissolution machine; and it has no standards for registration of malaria medicines. The WHO/USP assessment found that there was a severe need for equipment, supplies, and training at the national reference laboratory.

Cambodia
Western Cambodia has long been considered the epicenter of antimalarial drug resistance. One leading hypothesis of its etiology is the widespread use of falsified and substandard medicines. Since 2003, the USG has supported a drug surveillance network of "sentinel sites" in Cambodia to monitor the quality of antimalarial medicines in the private and public sectors. This support has included not only routine field monitoring, but also capacity building around drug quality issues with the Department of Drugs and Food, the Pharmacists' Association of Cambodia, and the National Malaria Center. In addition, several public awareness campaigns have been launched to educate clients about the dangers associated with the use of falsified medications.

Lao PDR, Thailand, Vietnam
These three countries have very active programs aimed at addressing the problems of sub-standard and counterfeit medications. Through the support of USG and other donors, these countries have developed extensive networks of sentinel sites using portable drug quality testing kits. In addition, USP has worked with national food and drug administrations, medicine regulatory agencies, and other authorities to develop appropriate enforcement approaches to regulate the drug industry. The countries also benefit from training obtained through Asian Network of Excellence in Quality Assurance of Medicines, a network of university pharmaceutical programs providing technical assistance within the region to develop national capacities for quality assurance/quality control, good manufacturing practices, and bioavailability testing.

China
Drug quality activities within China have been coordinated by Government of China officials and WHO. Some of the falsified antimalarials coming into the GMS have originated from China, and WHO, working with INTERPOL (with non-USG funding) and with national enforcement authorities, has been successful in cracking down on some of the producers. The PMI team will not provide funding on this issue, as the Government of China is conducting their own routine monitoring of drug quality.

Progress to Date:
Burma
USP has begun work in Burma with the collection of information on the country's medicine QA/QC systems that are intended to ensure quality of antimalarial medications passing through the public and private system. Sentinel survey protocols were developed and training was held on the use of the minilabs for field-based testing of medicines collected from a wide variety of

venues. Additional staff from the national Food and Drug Administration laboratories in Nay Pyi Taw and Mandalay were trained on compendial testing methods so that they could conduct confirmatory testing of medicines suspected of being falsified.

Cambodia

PMI continues to support the Cambodian Ministry of Health to monitor antimalarial drug quality and to take action when falsified or substandard medicines are found. USP worked closely with the Department of Drugs and Food and other local partners to ensure that Minilab reference standards were replenished and that regulatory authorities continued to make routine drug inspections and field visits. With assistance from PMI, the Department of Drugs and Food successfully launched raids on facilities selling unregistered and falsified antimalarial medications. Additionally, to ensure a continue stream of professionals aware of the problem with substandard and falsified medicines, USP supported the updating of QA/QC and medicine regulations curriculum for Cambodian pharmacy and medical students.

Regional, Lao PDR, Thailand, Vietnam

PMI has made tremendous strides towards establishing a drug quality network in the GMS, periodically collecting field specimens for monitoring of drug quality and working with national and international authorities to enforce drug manufacturing policies. USP has conducted site visits to Cambodia, Lao PDR, Thailand, and Vietnam to provide needed reagents, reference standards, USP-national formularies, and other essential supplies. USP is also providing technical guidance to the countries as appropriate and following up on actions taken by countries, e.g., in Cambodia, closing down outlets and in Laos, issuing regulatory notices, and fining and educating violators. They continue to strengthen medicine quality assurance systems through in-country capacity building. Technical assistance is provided to the National Health Products Quality Control Centers laboratories through advanced analytical trainings, provision of equipment and supplies, and ongoing good laboratory practices assistance to attain accreditation by the International Organization for Standardization.

Over the last year, PMI established two regional mechanisms to both promote information sharing among GMS countries. The Build Regional Expertise in Medicines Regulation, Information Sharing, Joint Investigation and Enforcement mechanism is designed to increase regional cooperation and access to pool of experts in medicines regulation to address the medicines quality issues and problems in the region. Through this mechanism, country medicine regulatory agencies and other law enforcement agencies would have regional platform for timely information sharing for effective enforcement beyond national and regional levels working in partnership with WHO (SEARO and WPRO), INTERPOL, ASEAN, and national authorities. The second mechanism is the Asia Pacific Network of Official Medicines Control Laboratories, which assists with QA/QC laboratories in the region to support regulatory authorities in controlling the quality of antimalarial medications available on the market. This new network parallels other successful Official Medicines Control Laboratories networks worldwide.

In the areas where sampling of drugs is ongoing a notable decrease in the presence of counterfeit or substandard malaria medications has been observed. According to data provided by USP, in 2003 the overall failure rate was 21.8%. The figures were 3.5%, 3.9%, 7.0%, 3.0%, 1.0%, 0.5%, and 1.3% for years 2005 through 2011. It is important to note, however, that these data were collected from a sample of sentinel sites only and may not represent the entire region.

China
There was no engagement with the sub-regional antimalarial drug quality program in China. Unfortunately, while there is support within certain sectors, introducing routine drug quality monitoring in the Yunnan Province of China continues to present challenges and USP has not been active in China since 2004. Though attempting to receive approval for activities for several years, they have yet to receive it from the State Food and Drug Administration in Beijing.

While significant advances in improving antimalarial drug quality have occurred (reported reductions in Cambodia, replacement of artemisinin monotherapy in Burma), overall the region continues to identify many non-compliant producers, distributors, and sellers. Efforts thus far have not been guided by a regional strategy. With FY 2013 funding, PMI plans to undertake a multi-country drug quality strategic assessment to review all efforts to date, including import controls, post-market surveillance, national and regional enforcement, development of laboratory capacity, political pressure, BCC, and public awareness. Given its importance for PMI investments, there will be particular focus on USP strategies and performance. The assessment will guide investments for both PMI and other donors during the coming period. This assessment is especially timely with the formation of the Global Fund's Regional Artemisinin Resistance Initiative that promises increased attention to the problem of sub-standard drugs, but does not yet have a plan of action. Stakeholders will be invited to provide input and share in the outcomes of this strategic assessment in order to develop a guiding document for PMI investments and other donors in the region.

Planned activities with FY 2014 funding ($350,000 Total: $50,000 Burma, $100,000 Cambodia, $200,000 Regional)

- **Support to maintain post-marketing surveillance:** PMI will continue ongoing support for the national medicines regulatory agencies to conduct post-marketing surveillance via the medicines quality monitoring network with improved dynamic sampling throughout the GMS. PMI will continue to support engagement at the regional level to enhance cooperation, training, investigation, and enforcement. PMI will continue to support the Asian Network of Excellence in Quality Assurance of Medicines in playing a key role in facilitating regional trainings. PMI-supported partners will to encourage "south-to-south" cooperation and scientific exchanges whenever possible. PMI will continue to work with other important partners in the region including the Global Fund, French Embassy, Lower Mekong Initiative, WHO, among others. PMI will work to ensure that national pharmaceutical reference laboratories are qualified to conduct the necessary analyses for pre- and post-marketing surveillance of drug quality, both for the timely and accurate analyses of samples from the medicines quality monitoring as well as samples collected through other investigations. This activity entails providing support to quality control laboratories toward achieving the ISO/IEC 17025 and/or WHO pre-qualification status allowing them to perform the analyses of all essential medicines, including those provided under the Global Fund grants. PMI will support the improvement of academic curriculum for pharmacy and medical students through the incorporation of relevant modules on QA/QC of medicines. This will equip the graduating students with the skills and knowledge of problems with medicine quality.

  a. **Burma:** support for drug quality monitoring. ($50,000)
  b. **Cambodia:** support for drug quality monitoring. ($100,000)
  c. **Regional:** support for regional drug quality monitoring including Thailand, Lao, and Vietnam. ($200,000)

BEHAVIOR CHANGE COMMUNICATION

PMI-supported malaria programs in the GMS are strategically focused on strengthening malaria prevention and case management along international border areas between Burma, Thailand and Cambodia concentrating in areas with evidence or threats of artemisinin resistance and hard-to-reach forests, foothills and recently cleared land for agricultural or industrial purposes. These are areas where transmission is high, health systems are weak, access to quality malaria services is difficult, and private drug sellers are often unregulated. Behavior change communication and social mobilization is an integral part of these interventions.

Target high-risk populations include local forest dweller residents, new settlers, internal and external migrant workers, and people crossing border areas. The PMI also prioritizes pregnant women and children under five years of age who are most vulnerable to malaria.

Key behaviors to influence include use of treated nets, prompt diagnosis and treatment of fever, adherence to treatments, and avoidance of monotherapies and counterfeit drugs. The ethnic and linguistic diversity of GMS, traditional beliefs related to causes of and remedies for malaria, and mobility of key target groups, present unusual challenges for BCC. Achieving these behavioral objectives requires not only appropriate BCC processes and approaches but also access to quality malaria services for internal mobile workers and registered and unregistered migrants crossing national boundaries. Thailand is a hub for migrant workers from neighboring countries and PMI supports Thailand's BVBD to increase access to malaria prevention and treatment for these migrant workers.

Dissemination of BCC messages are cross-cutting activities and integrated in prevention and promotion activities as well as treatment compliance counseling conducted by village malaria workers (VMWs) based in the communities. With the availability of LLINs, RDTs and ACTs at the facility level, BCC and social mobilization activities are designed to motivate targeted at-risk populations to access and utilize these interventions.

Burma
In 2007, WHO in collaboration with VBDC and other agencies working in malaria control developed a framework for BCC activities entitled *"Communication and Social Mobilization for Malaria Prevention and Control in Myanmar."* The strategy calls for the need to educate at-risk population that malaria is a life-threatening disease that can be prevented with ITNs and treated with ACTs. It encourages multi-sectoral partnerships to combat malaria involving opinion leaders, various groups of community leaders and collaboration from both public and private health services providers, and emphasizes the importance of engaging families and target

populations for action and behavior change in meaningful ways through interactive communication and counseling.

The WHO *Strategic Framework for Artemisinin Resistance Containment in Myanmar 2011-2015*, also identifies BCC as an integral part of all malaria interventions, serving to improve the utilization of available health services offering quality diagnostics and ACTs, reducing the demand for artemisinin monotherapies in the private sector, and improving adherence to the three-day ACT regimen. The framework echoed recommendations of the earlier communication strategy and suggested gathering information on BCC efforts targeting migrants in neighboring countries and ensuring consistent messaging. PMI communication strategy and plans implemented through PMI partners are aligned with these national BCC strategies, support and complement existing campaign efforts from national, regional to community levels.

Village health volunteers have been playing an important role in providing health education and key BCC messages on malaria prevention and early diagnosis and treatment in the target communities. As such, Burma has expanded the network of VHVs through the support of Global Fund Round 9, the implementation of MARC Framework, and the PMI.

Cambodia

To support the National Malaria Elimination Plan 2011-2025, the CNM launched a *"National Behavior Change Communication Strategy for Malaria Prevention and Control/Elimination Program, Cambodia"* in November 2012.Target populations included in the strategy are general population, internal mobile and migrant workers and people crossing national borders to and from neighboring countries. Three key objectives of the BCC interventions are to increase consistent use of ITNs among target communities, improve health seeking behaviors among at-risk populations and improve compliance to medication.

Cambodia stratifies malaria risks into three zones: zone 1 includes four provinces with evidence of artemisinin resistance, zone 2 contains nine high-risk provinces with some delay in parasite clearance, and zone 3 consists of 10 lower risk provinces in the eastern part of the country. With support from Global Fund, ITN distribution and subsidized treatment, the situation has been improved. However, with the evidence of artemisinin resistance along the Thai-Cambodian border, one of the main challenges is to reach mobile and migrant populations. Those at risk include people coming to work in endemic area as seasonal farm workers in large plantations and smaller farms as well as those who spend time in the forest for extended periods, such as gem miners, loggers, sandal wood collectors and soldiers. Behavior change communication activities conducted through radio and TV spots encourage use of appropriate preventive measures, stressing the importance of treating conventional bednets with insecticide and seeking early diagnosis and treatment, as well as rational drug use.

Regional

Thailand's Global Fund Round 10 aims to provide support for comprehensive BCC, community mobilization, and access to health services for both Thai and migrants residing in malaria transmission zones in 22 provinces bordering Thailand to its neighbors. The BVBD developed a framework for BCC for Thai population that encourages acceptance of IRS, prompt treatment-seeking behaviors, adherence to drug regimens, and usage of LLIN and LLHNs when staying outdoors.

The BCC component targeting displaced Burmese along the Thai-Burmese border and other migrant populations in Thailand is led by the International Organization for Migration which has conducted an assessment of migrant populations and developed a BCC strategy. The assessment found persisting misconceptions and limited understanding of malaria among displaced ethnic groups along the Thai-Burmese border, particular the Karen who have had little access to information and health education, while other migrant groups including the Mon, Pa-O, Lao and Cambodians are faring better.

PMI supports the BVBD to increase the availability of multi-lingual BCC materials appropriate for transnational migrants from other GMS countries to increase effective prevention, health-seeking behaviors and treatment compliance.

Progress to date:

Burma
PMI is focusing its support in Tanintharyi and Kayin regions adjacent to Thailand. These are Tier 1 and Tier 2 regions with high malaria transmission. To inform and gain support from relevant health authorities and other stakeholders during the start-up period in FY 2012, advocacy meetings were held to sensitize the health and administrative officials from state, township, and village levels on malaria situation and the project plans. In Kayin state, local Karen ethnic groups benefit from established community-based malaria interventions and community health worker networks that are integrated within the existing local health structure. These Community Health Groups support the work of trained VMWs. Besides administering RDTs and case management, the VMWs have been trained on community mobilization strategies, use of communication tools and bednet re-impregnation. Malaria education sessions have been conducted in the communities by VMWs with support from PMI project team. In Tanintharyi Division, the populations include local residents as well as large and small groups of internal migrants working in agricultural plantations and at the Dawei Deep Seaport Project. The geography comprises forests, mountainous terrains to the east and coastal land to the west. Mobile malaria education and clinic teams have been established and provided scheduled outreach malaria prevention campaigns and screening of febrile patient for treatment if found positive in the forests and foothills. PMI partners also work with business sector employers to strengthen and improve their malaria services for migrant workers.

As of March 2013, 276 PMI-supported VMWs have provided effective case management of malaria, conducted BCC, distributed LLINs and retreated bed nets. During October 2012 and March 2013, VMWs conducted 13,475 health education sessions through various events and activities reaching over 36,000 people. The VMWs distributed 39,716 LLINs in the target communities.

Cambodia
BCC and social mobilization activities have been scaled up in Cambodia building upon a previous USAID-supported project. Malaria education campaigns targeting local residents,

mobile seasonal workers, and people traveling into endemic areas have been conducted through various channels for reinforcement. During March and April before the rainy season, mobile campaign events took place in villages along border provinces jointly organized with local health authorities and VMWs. The event included a blood test with an RDT for any person with fever and treatment if the client was found positive, infotainment through video spots and feature film followed by quizzes, and free net retreatment. The campaigns help people to understand the importance of sleeping under ITN, the need to seek appropriate treatment immediately from VMWs, and the harm of counterfeit drugs.

Travelers into endemic zones receive and discuss malaria prevention issues and messages with trained taxi drivers participating with the program. VMWs give counseling and treatment services to patients and facilitate listener discussion-group during and after radio call-in show program. The show has been popular as it helped to answer questions right away and reach large audiences. Various communication tools for health workers have been produced and distributed to VMWs after BCC trainings. Malaria in pregnancy has started to gain attention in Cambodia and the CNM has provided guidance for malaria screening and treatment among pregnant women attending ANC in endemic areas. To raise awareness on vulnerability to malaria among pregnant women and children under five, the PMI BCC program has produced educational materials and posters for health workers and the general population. The PMI also trains pharmacies and drug sellers in cities and towns on rational drug use and set up referral system of those tested positive to nearest health facilities.

As of March 2013, PMI partners have trained and supported 505 VMWs and 78 migrant malaria workers (MMWs) in the 10 target operational districts of seven provinces. Mobile malaria campaigns took place in April around the Malaria Day event and mobile units traveled to 55 villages, working with local VMWs to hold the event. More than 6,000 people participated in these events that included retreating 1,684 conventional bed nets and screening and treating 303 people for malaria as part of an awareness campaign. During the same period, more than 37,000 passengers received malaria education from trained taxi drivers transporting them into the endemic areas.

Regional
In Thailand, a BCC technical working group has been established and includes representatives from BVBD, health communications specialists from Thai academia, WHO, Malaria Consortium, other NGO partners, and community members. In addition, a Migrant BCC Sub-Committee was also set up and led by BVBD and the International Organization for Migration. The migrant malaria and BCC assessment that had been conducted by that Organization formed the basis of a BCC strategy for short- and long-term migrant populations in Thailand. The strategy emphasizes friendly tools for semi-literate audience including pictures or graphics depicting living situations that the target groups can relate to with the content explaining the breeding environment, symptoms, the mechanism of mosquito bites and sickness in humans, effective prevention measures, the need to complete prescribed treatment, and that all messages should include clear and specific calls to action. The International Organization for Migration is in the process of developing a set of job aids and communication tools.

Cross-border collaboration in BCC and harmonization of messages has taken place between Thailand and Cambodia. Joint pre-testing of bi-lingual BCC materials were conducted in Pailin and Chanthaburi and resulted in improvement of the ACT instruction and net treatment posters for use by VMWs and at health posts and clinics.

PMI is supporting the NMCP in Lao PDR to respond to the recent outbreak of malaria cases in six southern provinces. PMI supported an assessment of the outbreak in early 2013. The assessment found poor health-seeking behaviors and low knowledge of malaria. According to the report, local inhabitants still link malaria with poverty, drinking unclean water and poor hygiene, while self-medication with a packet of mixed medicines was common and patients usually wait two days before going to VHVs or health center for diagnosis and treatment. The assessment recommends conducting BCC campaigns to improve preventive and treatment seeking behaviors, building diagnosis and case management capacity and making RDTs, ACTs and LLINs available at the community level.

With FY 2013 funding, PMI plans to undertake a BCC assessment in three countries (Burma, Cambodia and Thailand) to better understand progress to date and identify remaining gaps to strengthening BCC efforts. PMI has supported specific intervention approaches, focusing on defined geographical areas along the borders of Cambodia, Thailand and Burma, and targeting special populations who frequently travel in and out of the endemic areas. As such, the PMI supported interventions have developed special BCC approaches and messages intended to reach and influence these at-risk populations. Besides PMI, the national malaria control programs in these three countries and their implementing partners have also implemented various BCC strategies and activities with other donor support. The proposed assessment will review: national BCC strategies and guidelines of Cambodia, Thailand and Burma; the quality and availability of BCC training and materials; existing approaches, messages, tools and job aids being disseminated and utilized on the ground by different projects, and the extent to which the target mobile/migrant populations and local residents are being reached. The report will provide recommendations on how BCC and social mobilization activities can be strengthened, delivered more effectively, and messages harmonized within and among the three countries.

Planned activities with FY 2014 funding ($125,000 Total: $100,000 Cambodia, $25,000 Thailand)

The PMI supported malaria interventions in the GMS serve to strengthen, enhance, and fill gaps of national programs and activities being funded by other donors, particularly the Global Fund. Major communication and social mobilization efforts with FY 2014 funding will attempt to further increase culturally appropriate BCC materials, approaches and channels; improve interpersonal communication skills and techniques of malaria volunteers and health educators working in the communities, and that of health staff working at health facility level; and harmonize the key prevention and treatment messages among the PMI focus countries including limited support for Lao PDR, and training of new malaria workers and volunteers on health communication as the program expands its coverage in Burma and Cambodia. In line with NMCP strategies, PMI supports two VMWs per village in Cambodia and one VHW per village in Burma. Emphasis will be given to interpersonal and group communication up to 70% of BCC efforts. Support will include training and disseminating of already developed BCC materials on malaria prevention, accurate diagnosis, and prompt and effective treatment. PMI-supported BCC activities include:

- **Community-level prevention activities including distribution and promotion of LLINs:** PMI will support the distribution and promotion of LLIN use among targeted populations in focus areas in Burma, Cambodia and Thailand. The costs of the distribution and LLIN promotion include BCC activities to augment malaria prevention efforts implemented by community health/malaria volunteers in the focus areas and engage community members and networks, including employers of migrant and forest workers, to raise awareness about malaria and use of preventive measures. (BCC costs for Burma are included under the LLIN section.)

- **Case management at the community level, including implementation, training and supervision:** PMI will support training and supervision of VMWs and private sector providers in Cambodia and Burma and provide technical support for malaria posts and malaria volunteers in Thailand. As part of their training and supervision, PMI will support BCC activities to strengthen their interpersonal counseling and communication skills, adapt and disseminate culturally appropriate BCC materials through the network of health volunteers, educate private providers about correct treatment and diagnosis and the harm of using monotherapy and sub-standard drugs, and develop mass media messages to reach specific target populations including migrants and mobile populations. (BCC costs for Burma, Cambodia and Thailand are included under the case management section.)

- **Behavior change communication technical assistance for community-level implementation**: To ensure harmonization and dissemination of BCC materials and messages in the three focus countries (Burma, Cambodia, and Thailand), PMI will support development and implementation of effective BCC approaches. Careful consideration will be given to special and high risk target groups with BCC approaches focused on improving coverage and use of malaria prevention measures (LLINs, hammocks, retreatment kits), and increase awareness of malaria in pregnancy, dangers of counterfeit antimalarials, as well as prompt diagnosis and effective treatment.
    a. **Cambodia:** strengthening community-level BCC implementation. ($100,000)
    b. **Thailand:** strengthening community-level BCC implementation. ($25,000)

MONITORING AND EVALUATION

PMI will focus on the following M&E areas: 1) ensuring the collection of quality, standardized routine data and survey data from the cross-border focus areas that feeds into national surveillance systems; 2) development of one national M&E plan for each country; 3) provision of technical support for national/sub-national surveys; and 4) strengthening national M&E capacity.

Efforts to strengthen malaria control in areas with evidence of artemisinin resistance will be targeted to cross-border focus areas where PMI will deliver community-level interventions and contribute to achieving the sub-regional targets set by WHO of reducing malaria morbidity and mortality by 50% by 2015 compared to 2010. Depending on partners' access and resources, PMI will explore extending its geographic reach to other areas of threatened artemisinin resistance. Support is provided to strengthen M&E activities in the cross-border focus areas, to strengthen routine data collection at the community level, and track several outcome indicators through periodic surveys. The coverage targets will be set higher (100% ITN ownership and 90% use) than previous PMI targets, as the areas with documented artemisinin resistance require intensive scale-up (See Goals and Targets). The PMI targets are consistent with the targets set by the program for their containment zones. Reaching and maintaining these ambitious targets will require sustained commitment and financing.

Burma

The current National Strategic Plan for Malaria Prevention and Control 2010-2015 aims to achieve the Millennium Development Goals. Their M&E plan focuses on collecting 20 indicators through both routine reporting and periodic surveys. These indicators are consistent with the PMI indicators. Their current public sector malaria information system involves basic health staff submitting monthly reports to their respective Township Health Department which then forwards the report to the State/Regional VBDC Office. The State/Regional VBDC Team then analyzes the data on a quarterly basis and sends feedback to the Township level. This system is paper-based and there are major challenges with data flow and analysis. Furthermore, the current system does not effectively capture information from the private sector or NGOs. Burma conducted a sub-national malaria survey in 2011-2012 in containment zones 1 & 2 as part of the MARC project, but there has not been a national malaria survey that includes coverage estimates and malaria biomarkers.

Efforts to strengthen malaria control in areas with evidence of artemisinin resistance will be targeted to cross-border focus areas of Tanintharyi, Kayin, and southern Rakhine States. PMI is collecting routine surveillance data from these focus areas and a survey was completed to collect baseline coverage estimates.

Cambodia

Cambodia's 2011-2025 National Strategic Plan for Elimination of Malaria has set a national elimination goal of 2025. The Cambodian national program prioritizes data collection through a variety of methodologies, including routine monitoring, baseline, mid-term and end-line quantitative and qualitative surveys. The health information system, malaria information system and community surveillance data (generated through the VMW project) will determine impact on malaria burden in the different provinces. The Cambodian national program reports to the Health Sector Support Project every quarter on a set of mutually agreed coverage and impact indicators. They also submit to the Planning Department of the Ministry of Health data pertaining to malaria incidence rate, malaria mortality rate and malaria case fatality rate. The current surveillance system does not pool the facility-based data reporting to the malaria information system with the community level data reported by the VMWs. Most importantly, private sector data is currently not collected and thus not reported. Cambodia has conducted longitudinal national malaria surveys in 2004, 2007, and 2010. These data have shown decreasing malaria prevalence by microscopy as well as sero-prevalence and increasing ITN coverage. Plans to repeat these surveys in 2012 and 2014 have been delayed.

Efforts to strengthen malaria control in areas with evidence of artemisinin resistance will be targeted to fourteen focus operational districts along Cambodia's borders with Thailand, Lao PDR and Vietnam. The PMI is collecting routine surveillance data from these focus areas and a survey was completed to collect baseline coverage estimates.

Regional

Thailand's 2011-2016 National Strategic Plan for Malaria Control and Elimination sets as their target malaria elimination in 80% of the country by the year 2020. Lao PDR's 2011-2015 National Strategy for Malaria Control and Pre-Elimination sets goals of reducing incidence and deaths and reaching pre-elimination. Vietnam's 2012-2015 National Strategic Plan aims to reduce morbidity and mortality and achieve malaria elimination in 34 provinces. Malaria has been integrated into the HMIS in all six GMS countries. The HMIS and its capacity in the GMS vary widely from paper to web-based surveillance and from passive case detection (of cases that may or may not be parasitologically confirmed) to active case detection in some places e.g. China and containment zones of Thailand and Cambodia. Limitations include delays and incompleteness of reporting and the collection of data only from the public sector. Most programs struggle to collect data from peripheral settings, such as from Village Health Volunteers, the private sector, the military, and migrants. Routine surveillance challenges in the region include a lack of adequate feedback and supervision, poor information technology structures limiting timely reporting of data, and weak capacity for data management and analysis, especially at the periphery. Often the data is not disaggregated by factors that are epidemiologically pertinent (e.g. age, gender, pregnancy status, ethnicity, migrant status, or occupation). These weaknesses were highlighted in the delay of identifying a recent malaria outbreak in the southern provinces of Lao PDR reporting caseloads four to eight times the previous year's levels.

Thailand has completed its first national malaria survey and the results are pending. Lao PDR has conducted a DHS with a malaria module, but the results are not yet available.

Efforts to strengthen malaria control in areas with evidence of artemisinin resistance will be targeted to cross-border focus areas of Trat/Chantaburi and Ranong, Thailand. PMI is collecting routine surveillance data from these focus areas and a survey was completed to collect baseline coverage estimates.

Progress to Date:

Monitoring and Evaluation table

Data Source	Geographic Area	Year					
		2010	2011	2012	2013	2014	2015
Household Surveys[1]	Burma		MARC (zone 1& 2)*	CAP-M baseline	MARC (?)		DHS (?)

	Cambodia	Malaria National Survey* DHS*	ACT Watch HH* CAP-M baseline	CAP-M baseline	Malaria National Survey (?)		DHS (?)
	Regional		Lao DHS* (2011-12)	Thai CAP-M baseline	Thai national malaria survey		
Other Surveys[2]	**Burma**						
	Cambodia	Migrant RDS survey at Thai border*	ACT Watch Outlet*	ACT Watch Supply Chain Report* FHI 360 migrant survey in Pailin*			
	Regional	Migrant RDS survey at Thai-Cambodia border*		Migrant RDS survey at Thai-Burma border			
Other Data Sources[4]	**Burma**	TES	Ento monitoring; TES; TRaC*	Ento monitoring; TES; TRaC;* Drug quality monitoring	Ento monitoring TES TRaC* Drug quality monitoring	Ento monitoring; TES; LLIN durability monitoring; Drug quality monitoring	
	Cambodia	TES	Ento monitoring TES Drug Quality Monitoring TRaC*	Ento monitoring TES Drug Quality Monitoring TRaC*	Ento monitoring TES Drug Quality Monitoring TRaC*	Ento monitoring TES Drug Quality Monitoring	

Regional	TES	Ento monitoring TES Drug Quality Monitoring TRaC*	Ento monitoring TES Drug Quality Monitoring TRaC*	Ento monitoring TES Drug Quality Monitoring TRaC*	Ento monitoring TES Drug Quality Monitoring	

* Not PMI-supported

Burma

Burma recently completed a sub-national survey that includes malaria intervention coverage and prevalence estimates in the MARC areas, which overlaps with PMI focus areas. Monitoring and evaluation of PMI's activities in the cross-border focus areas is multi-pronged with collection of routine data and survey data in the project areas. The majority of the indicators to be monitored by PMI will come from routine surveillance data except for key ITN ownership and use numbers. PMI is supporting a surveillance system assessment which will provide recommendations for strengthening routine surveillance. PMI engages with the formal private sector to improve case management and malaria reporting. This is in its nascent phase of mapping the registered private providers.

The CAP-Malaria project continues to collect routine malaria surveillance data at the community level. This includes Day 3 positive surveillance at sentinel sites. A baseline survey has been completed for the cross-border focus areas.

Cambodia

PMI is assisting the CNM to develop an electronic Malaria Information System that incorporates health facility and community-level village malaria worker malaria data. This system was designed to include relevant program data (e.g. bednet distribution, malaria drug and diagnostic stock and listing of private sector providers) and link to the general health information system for comparison. CNM has recently posted this pilot on-line (http://www.cnm.gov.kh/index.php?action=ID80). The malaria surveillance data underestimate the true burden since the majority of malaria treatment occurs in the private sector. PMI engages with the formal private sector to improve case management and malaria reporting. To improve collection of data from migrants and mobile populations, a cadre of Mobile Malaria Workers specifically targeting mobile/migrant populations has been deployed and their malaria data is now incorporated into the malaria surveillance system.

The CAP-Malaria project continues to collect routine malaria surveillance data at the community level. This includes Day 3 positive surveillance in pilot villages with follow-up response entailing screening for additional malaria infections around the index case and on a limited basis IRS. A baseline survey has been completed for the cross-border focus areas.

Regional

Malaria Consortium is supporting Thailand as they seek to streamline their surveillance system and transition to a smartphone-based reporting and alert system. In response to increasing malaria cases in southern Laos, PMI supported an outbreak investigation which was led by CMPE with support from WHO, Centers for Disease Control and Prevention, and Malaria Consortium. The team concluded that there was sufficient data to confirm that malaria has surpassed epidemic thresholds in the southern provinces, with the predominant species being *P. falciparum*, and the demographic most affected being males over 5 years of age. Given frequent cross-border migrations for work to nearby provinces with known artemisinin resistance and inadequate surveillance of migrant populations, the team made several recommendations e.g. improving delivery of malaria commodities, engagement with private employers, increasing BCC activities and building case management and malaria reporting capacity of community malaria workers.

Malaria data from migrants and mobile populations have been difficult to ascertain as traditional survey methods may miss this population and routine surveillance data varies as to the collection of this demographic information. The PMI-supported respondent-driven sampling survey, a methodology used often with hidden populations, amongst Burmese migrants to ascertain malaria prevention and treatment coverage and prevalence estimates has been completed in Ranong, Thailand. This migrant survey noted very low malaria prevalence amongst these Burmese migrants and noted lower ITN utilization than reported for Thai residents.

To assist NMCPs to adopt the regional M&E indicators and to build M&E capacity, a regional M&E course was conducted in October 2011 and in September 2012. The curriculum developed by the M&E technical partners led by Malaria Consortium/CDC aims to train a cadre of M&E experts and trainers within each country who would be able to adapt the curriculum to their country context and conduct national and sub-national trainings. Following the training, Lao PDR has adapted the curriculum to their national context and has conducted provincial-level trainings.

WHO continues to update the regional strategic document, Mekong Malaria III, which includes both epidemiological and entomological data and analyses on relationships with health systems, program costs and financing, community involvement, private sector engagement, and cross-border collaboration. This analytical review also projects regional trends in socio-economic development, migration, and other factors likely to affect malaria transmission.

Planned activities with FY 2014 funding ($924,000 total: $662,000 Burma, $100,000 Cambodia, $162,000 Regional)

- **Support for M&E activities and surveillance strengthening**: Support will be provided in revising national strategic plans as well as updating national M&E plans. Technical assistance will be provided to ensure quality routine surveillance and survey data collection that have been harmonized with other regional efforts.
    a. **Burma:** Development of a data management and analysis platform to improve public sector reporting that can also encompass malaria data from various non-public sectors e.g. private sector and NGOs. ($100,000)
    b. **Cambodia:** Efforts will focus on combining data from the health facilities and the village malaria workers as well as building on the current web-based reporting system to

incorporate data from the private sector and mobile and migrant populations. PMI will support CNM in coordinating their M&E work stream. ($100,000)

   c. **Regional:** Limited technical assistance will be provided for countries as they adapt the regional M&E curriculum and conduct in-country cascade training. Technical assistance will be provided as needed to assist with outbreak investigations and conduct situational analyses. ($150,000)

- **National Malaria Household Survey 2014/2015:** A nationally representative household survey to collect malaria intervention coverage estimates and malaria parasitemia data.
  - a. **Burma:** There are on-going discussions regarding the best survey tool (e.g. DHS, MIS, or MARC survey) to support VBDC and the various donor needs. PMI will provide technical assistance and funding support to ensure coordination and possible oversampling of the PMI project areas. ($500,000)

- **Private sector malaria data collection:** Although the majority of patients seek malaria treatment in the private sector especially in Cambodia and Burma, this data is currently not captured. To accurately determine malaria morbidity and mortality and to track the progress made with the scale-up of malaria interventions, it is crucial to improve malaria case management with a focus on parasitological diagnosis and to track that data in the private sector.
  - a. **Burma:** As PMI begins to focus on quality assurance of case management services in the private sector, the collection of malaria data will also be incorporated. (See case management section)
  - b. **Cambodia:** The PMI will provide targeted support to improve case management quality assurance activities in the private sector as well as developing and implementing a reporting system to capture malaria confirmed case information, which will eventually be incorporated into the Cambodian national malaria surveillance system. (See case management section)

- **Technical assistance on M&E:** A CDC medical epidemiologist will provide technical assistance with on-going M&E activities, provide input on planned surveys, and support NMCP's with their M&E plans.
  - a. **Burma:** A CDC TDY to support M&E activities e.g. the national survey. ($12,000)
  - b. **Regional:** A CDC TDY to support M&E activities e.g. surveillance assessments or outbreak investigations. ($12,000)

Surveillance: Drug resistance and therapeutic efficacy studies

Therapeutic efficacy studies (TES) and other drug resistance monitoring methods have played a critical role in the detection of resistance to several classes of malaria drugs. Previous USAID and PMI investments in this area supported the creation of the bi-regional WHO Mekong Malaria Program, which continues to provide technical assistance throughout the six countries comprising the GMS. The PMI-supported GMS TES network comprises of 35 sentinel sites that are active in the six countries on a rotating basis (Cambodia- 5 sites; China- 3 sites in Yunnan; Lao PDR- 3 sites; Burma- 10 sites; Thailand- 9 sites; Vietnam- 5 sites). This network has been strengthened in the past few years to include chloroquine-resistant *P. vivax* monitoring and to extend its geographic coverage. Therapeutic efficacy studies have played a crucial role in shaping NMCP treatment policies. In 2008, Thailand's treatment policy shifted from a two- to three-day regimen in response to suboptimal clinical responses documented in Trat, and now has shifted to DHA-Pip in response to preliminary data obtained from TES sites along the Thai-Burma border. In Cambodia, similar data prompted a shift away from artesunate-mefloquine, to DHA-Pip (for treatment of both *P. falciparum* and *vivax* infections), and finally to use of Malarone in Pailin.

In addition to the value of determining clinical outcomes, the TES protocols are also useful for determining parasitological markers that may presage inadequate clinical responses. The persistence of parasitemia at the third day after treatment ("D3 positives") has been proposed as a potential marker of possible foci of artemisinin resistance and could be effective tracked in settings where prolonged patient follow up may not be necessary, or where logistical impediments preclude the conduct of formal *in vivo* studies. Another benefit of D3 positivity as a marker of resistance is that it may be more reflective of inadequate drug responses to the artemisinin component of an ACT regimen. Although there are not yet data to rigorously correlate D3 positivity to clinical outcomes, it is generally acknowledged that patients without D3 parasitemia are likely to achieve cure. Hence, the true value of D3 parasite measurements may be in determining where it is absent, thus allowing for prioritization of malaria control resources elsewhere.

Progress to Date:
The regional GMS TES network meeting was held in June 2012. Participants included representatives from each of the six GMS countries; meeting activities included reviewing the latest TES data, drafting plans for future TES studies in2014, and reviewing QA/AC practices to ensure reliability of TES results. Results disseminated at that meeting[9] showed that artemether-lumefantrine and DHA-Pip are both highly efficacious in Lao PDR and China where they are first-line treatments, respectively. Preliminary analyses indicate that the efficacy of DHA-Pip has declined below 80% in western Cambodia. In Thailand, efficacy of artesunate-mefloquine in Kanchanaburi and Ranong Provinces was 87% and 87-90%, respectively. In Burma, cure rates of 92-100% were seen in all TES sites against AL, DHA-Pip and A+M, and in Vietnam, DHA-Pip also remained efficacious with parasite clearance rates >96% in Gia Lai and Binh Phuoc.

---

[9]SEA-MAL 270 TES Workshop Kunming China

Percentage of treatment failure of different ACTs
in Greater Mekong Sub-region, 2006-2012

Analysis of D3 positivity data in TES sites was consistent with its role as a marker of artemisinin resistance. In western Cambodia, high proportions of D3 positivity were seen in Pailin (52%) and Pursat (36%), but not in eastern Cambodia. In Kanchanaburi Province, Thailand, increasing proportions of patients are still positive on D3, and in Vietnam, despite the fact that DHA-Pip efficacy remains high. Day3 positivity was observed in 15.3% and 11.3% of patients in Binh Phuoc and Gia Lai, respectively.

Although these sentinel sites have now been maintained for several years and remain a priority of the NMCPs, the network continues to strive for standardization of methods to ensure that results achieved throughout the network are truly generalizable. A major goal for the network will be to continue to ensure quality results among all participating sites. . Despite the fact that TESs present significant logistical and technical challenges, PMI will work with other partners with the aim of assuring that TES studies within the network can be compared to results from non-GMS sites. PMI will also attempt to ensure that both TES and regionally relevant entomologic surveillance are coordinated between GMS countries.

Planned activities with FY 2014 funding are as follows: ($1,054,000Total: $200,000 Burma, $250,000 Cambodia, $180,000 Thailand, $424,000 Regional)

- **Regional TES network:** PMI will continue to support the NMCPs to conduct therapeutic efficacy studies at 35 sites across the six countries. Along with testing the current first-line regimens, testing replacement therapies is imperative, especially as countries prepare to update their treatment guidelines. WHO will continue to provide regional coordination and technical assistance to the NMCPs in protocol adaptation, data analysis and dissemination of results, as well as updating national treatment guidelines.

  a. **Burma:** Support for in country designated TES sites, technical assistance for WHO investigator, monitoring, and biannual TES meeting ($200,000)

  b. **Cambodia:** Support for in country designated TES sites, technical assistance for WHO investigator, monitoring, and biannual TES meeting ($250,000)

  c. **Regional:** Support for designated TES sites in Laos, China and Vietnam; technical assistance from WHO investigator, monitoring, and biannual TES meeting ($424,000)

- **Thailand TES MOH Field sites:** PMI will maintain TES sentinel field sites in Thailand. ($120,000)

- **Support for Thailand BVBD TES activities:** PMI will build NMCP capacity to conduct TES in compliance with International Conference for Harmonization Good Clinical Practice guidance. ($60,000)

Surveillance: Entomology

As rapid ecologic changes occur with economic development, deforestation, and scale-up of LLINs in this sub-region, there is an urgent need to collect up-to-date, standardized data. The forested areas and possibly some plantations in the GMS are home to the region's most efficient malaria vector, *An. dirus*, with a second major vector, *An. minimus*, found in the forest and forest-fringe areas and possibly in the new orchard and rubber plantation ecologies. Beyond these two major vectors, there are a plethora of secondary vectors, whose importance in the rapidly changing ecology of the region is still largely unknown. Unlike the TES network, the entomological surveillance undertaken by NMCPs and some foundations, universities and research institutions within each of the GMS countries is often uncoordinated and the results are not widely disseminated.

Given the high donor investments in LLINs, studies assessing the physical and insecticidal durability of LLINs are needed. Such studies are currently on-going in Africa with PMI funds, but none have been conducted nor are currently planned in the GMS. With the launch of PMI and the community-level interventions in the region, PMI should develop appropriate methodologies for how durability studies should be done in the GMS.

Progress to Date:
A regional workshop was convened to monitor insecticide resistance and mapping of malaria vectors in the GMS in March 2012, with PMI support and in collaboration with WHO-Western Pacific and Southeast Asian Regional Offices. The workshop was attended by 40 representatives from participating GMS countries as well as observers-instructors from ten institutions. Outcomes included the development of country work plans for insecticide resistance monitoring and vector mapping, and an inventory of resources for entomologic monitoring in the GMS. An RBM meeting on Outdoor Malaria Transmission in Mekong Countries was held in Bangkok, March 2013, attended by 28 representatives from GMS countries and observers-presenters. Outcomes included the exchange of information and experiences on outdoor transmission in the GMS and development of protocols to assess efficacy and impact of control/preventive methods on outdoor transmission, with a focus on approaches to contain and eliminate foci of multidrug

resistance in Mekong countries. The PMI will continue to support regional strengthening of entomologic surveillance, insecticide resistance monitoring, and development and evaluation of methods to interrupt outdoor transmission. Working in collaboration with WHO and RBM , PMI will continue assisting with coordination of personnel and resources to strengthen entomologic monitoring in the region. PMI will also continue to engage with the Japan International Cooperation Agency, Mahidol University, Institute of Tropical Medicine Antwerp and the Armed Forces Research Institute of Medical Services to strengthen entomologic capacity in the region. PMI will support an entomology workshop planned for Burma, August 26 – September 6, 2013, to train NMCP staff in vector surveillance and control.

In the cross-border focus areas, where PMI and other donors are supporting efforts to scale up LLINs, NMCPs need to monitor and evaluate a few basic entomological parameters. In light of the changing ecologies, there are five areas of entomological monitoring that need to be addressed:

1. Location of the vectors, particularly in areas that have been deforested for farming or for orchards and rubber plantations, which may mimic the original forest ecology.

2. Vector biting time and place in relation to humans, and the potential impact of treated nets on these behaviors.

3. Insecticide resistance (limited studies suggest that pyrethroid resistance does not appear widespread).

4. Role of personal protection 'outside the house' such as treated hammocks and hammock nets, treated clothing and temporary shelters, and topical and spatial repellents to interrupt outdoor transmission.

5. Physical durability and insecticide retention of LLINs and treated materials.

Proposed USG activities with FY 2014 funding: ($417,000 total: $223,000 Burma, $149,000 Cambodia, $45,000 Regional)

- **Determination of vector transmission ecology in relation to current LLIN deployments in cross-border focus areas:** PMI will support entomological monitoring in the cross-border focus areas in coordination with the NMCPs and implementing partners. In these focus areas, the following primary entomological indicators will be collected: 1) species of malaria vectors in intervention areas; 2) vector distribution and seasonality; 3) vector feeding time and location; and 4) insecticide susceptibility and mechanisms of action.
  a. **Burma:** Entomologic surveillance.
     o **Entomologic surveillance (basic package):** Support of entomological at sentinel sites and insectary support in Rangoon. ($90,000)
     o **Supplies:** Expendable supplies and reagents for entomologic surveillance at sentinel sites in Burma, as well as supplies for the insectary in Rangoon.($10,000)
  b. **Cambodia:** Support of entomological at sentinel sites and insectary support in Cambodia. ($125,000)
  c. **Regional:** Support of entomological at sentinel sites in Thailand. ($35,000)

- **LLIN monitoring and durability:** Replacement policies in the GMS are usually based on LLINs lasting at least three-five years. PMI-funded studies in sub-Saharan Africa indicate that LLINs in some location have significant numbers of holes 6-12 months after being deployed, which may compromise effectiveness.

    a. **Burma:** PMI will support assessment of physical durability and insecticide retention of LLINs in Burma. A standard protocol developed for assessment for use in PMI-Africa countries will be modified to meet needs in Burma. ($100,000)

- **Insecticide resistance coordination.**
    a. **Regional:** Coordination of insecticide resistance monitoring activities in the region and information sharing. ($10,000)

- **Technical support for entomological studies and training.**
    a. **Burma:** Two CDC TDYs. ($23,000)
    b. **Cambodia:** Two CDC TDYs. ($24,000)

Operations Research

The GMS faces challenges of exploring different surveillance strategies for lower transmission and elimination settings, mounting a response to artemisinin resistance, outdoor transmission, high proportions of mixed infections, and the safe use of primaquine. Operations research will be essential in assessing innovative preventive and curative interventions and subsequent scale-up of these interventions in the Mekong context. Although numerous research partners exist in the region, OR priorities must be framed to directly inform control policies.

To identify the priority OR questions for the GMS, an OR symposium was convened for the sub-region in 2010. Prior to the symposium, country-level assessments of current OR activities, priorities, and gaps were identified and synthesized for the regional meeting. This regional symposium facilitated the development of an OR framework for malaria control and elimination in the GMS, by identifying common regional malaria research priorities, facilitating linkages across the region, and promoting greater coordination and sharing of findings. The symposium identified several priority questions for six topic areas (vector control and prevention, case management, *P. vivax* and safe use of primaquine, vulnerable populations, M&E and surveillance, and health systems and private sector).

The Joint Assessment of the Response to Artemisinin Resistance in the GMS funded by AusAID and BMGF identified the following priority areas for OR: a strategy on the addition of primaquine to ACT for treatment of *P. falciparum*, a field-ready test for G6PD deficiency, molecular markers for resistance, personal protective measures, *in vitro* susceptibility monitoring, highly sensitive diagnostic tools for detecting low-density parasitemia, patterns of population movement and expanded research into new drugs. Similarly, the recently published Emergency Response to Artemisinin Resistance in the Greater Mekong Sub-region identified the following high priority research topics: 1) mass drug administration for elimination of artemisinin-resistant parasites; 2) personal protection for special population groups; 3) use of gametocytocidal drugs; 4) reliable diagnostic tools for low-density parasitemia; 5) molecular marker for artemisinin resistance: and 6) modeling of multiple first-line therapies. In line with all these recent assessments on priority research, PMI has focused on research to address the safe deployment of primaquine and on potential interventions for outdoor transmission.

Progress to Date:

Burma

The RBM Vector Control Working Group established a network for outdoor transmission research in the Mekong countries and convened a meeting in March 2012 to discuss the strategic direction for research and development along the lines of entomological efficacy and community acceptability. With FY 2012 funds, an evaluation of insecticide-treated materials (e.g. vests/ longyis) amongst rubber tappers was submitted to the PMI OR committee. A scoping mission to inform the selection of clothing materials as well as the study design was recently completed. With FY 2013 funding, an evaluation of spatial repellents was proposed, but the specific study objectives and design are still pending.

Cambodia

With FY 2011 funding, PMI is supporting an evaluation of a point-of-care RDT (AccessBio) to assess for G6PD deficiency. A point-of-care test that could safely guide treatment with primaquine both for the clearance of *P. falciparum* gametocytes as well as for the prevention of relapses by *P. vivax* will have tremendous programmatic implications. An evaluation of a first generation RDT in Cambodia noted unacceptably low sensitivity and falsely diagnosed as normal a small percentage of persons with severely low levels of G6PD enzyme. In light of this disappointing data, PMI is supporting the evaluation of the third generation RDT to assess the test performance and ease of use. This study has completed field sample collection and results will be available shortly.

With FY 2012 funding, we have proposed to assess primaquine safety. In the Mekong with artemisinin resistance, there is evidence that patients with delayed parasite clearance have higher gametocyte carriage, thus an intervention to render these gametocytes non-infectious could be an important tool in the response to artemisinin resistance by curtailing the transmission of artemisinin-resistant strains. Although WHO has issued new recommendation to widely use a lower dose (0.25mg/kg) of primaquine without prior G6PD testing, CNM is hesitant to implement this dose without further safety data. We have submitted to PMI OR committee a study to follow hematologic outcomes after the administration of single-dose primaquine in G6PD-deficient falciparum malaria patients. This data if proven to be safe will provide CNM the evidence to widely implement this globally recommended strategy.

Proposed PMI activities with FY 2014 funding: ($87,000 Cambodia)

- **Personal Protection Evaluation:** Following the recommendations of the RBM Vector Control Working Group Outdoor Transmission Network on the strategic direction for research, PMI will support a project to assess the entomologic efficacy of personal protection measures such as permethrin-treated clothing, dichlorovos (Vapona Insect Strips), C8910 (a short-chain fatty acid-based spatial/area repellent) or other new spatial repellents to protect from outdoor and early biting vector mosquitoes.

a. **Cambodia:** Candidate personal protection items will be tested for user acceptability and feasibility, or possibly efficacy amongst target populations. The study will follow on to an FY13 pilot entomology study designed to down select personal protective measures in target populations. ($75,000)

- **Net User Preference assessment.**

    a. **Cambodia:** PMI will support efforts in Cambodia to assess current net use and preferences to guide LLIN procurement and retreatment policy (See ITN section).

- **Technical assistance with OR:** A CDC medical epidemiologist or entomologist will provide technical assistance for the design, implementation, or completion of the PMI OR activity.

    a. **Cambodia:** One CDC TDY ($12,000)

CAPACITY BUILDING

Malaria specific healthcare capacities in GMS countries face many challenges including the shortage of skilled health workers and technical staff, high turnover and lack of motivation among trained staff in remote and inaccessible areas. Decentralization of the health care system and integration of malaria control into general health services places an additional management burden on the provincial and district levels, where the disease presents in highest numbers. Despite limited resources, PMI will continue to support the system-wide capacity and health systems issues throughout the sub-region so long as those capacities have a malaria-specific purpose. PMI has provided long-standing support to strengthen regional technical capacity through the Asian Collaborative Training Network for Malaria or, ACT Malaria. ACT Malaria is an inter-country training and communication network which includes NMCPs of Bangladesh, Cambodia, China, Republic of Indonesia, Lao PDR, Malaysia, Burma, Philippines, Thailand, Timor-Leste, and Vietnam. ACT Malaria has been a primary mechanism for building technical and management capacity and facilitating information exchange among its member countries. Although PMI supports much of ACT Malaria's management costs, many trainees receive domestic or Global Fund support to participate in the organized courses. ACT Malaria is also a key partner in capacity building within the Asian Pacific Malaria Elimination Network which is supported by AusAID. While continuing their work with established courses e.g. the Management of Malaria Field Operations, Quality Assurance for Diagnostics, and Integrated Vector Management, ACT Malaria will explore opportunities to develop new curricula as identified by the executive board of the eleven member NMCPs.

Another PMI capacity building initiative capitalizes on the strength of the Thai MOPH Field Epidemiology Training Program, established with CDC technical assistance. Since 1998, Thailand has offered the International Field Epidemiology Training Program(FETP) to trainees from neighboring countries. To date, the program has produced over 100 FETP graduates, the majority of whom are now working in the MOPH, both at central and provincial levels. PMI plans to support one to two Burmese FETP residents in FY 2013 with professional support, including malaria projects that will provide professional experience with training and educational value. The FETP is a two year, full-time, postgraduate competency-based training program and is best described as "on-the-job training." Trainees will begin the FETP program in Thailand for 6 months, followed by an 18-month period back at their respective positions in NMCP. Training activities include conducting the outbreak investigations, evaluating surveillance systems, and conducting malaria field surveys in a "real life "malaria endemic area. Graduates earn a Certificate of Accomplishment in International Field Epidemiology Training Program – Thailand.

Progress to Date:
PMI continues to support regional training courses to build the capacity of NMCPs in the management of malaria field operations, M&E, diagnostics and case management and integrated vector management. Working through the Burma NMCP and MOPH, PMI has identified two candidates to undergo training in the Thailand FETP program anticipated to begin in the summer of 2013. Since the FETP program focus on all disease areas, a malaria-specific curriculum is currently under development by CDC Malaria Branch and will be integrated with the existing FETP program.

Planned activities with FY 2014 funding: ($500,000 Total: $150,000 Burma, $75,000 Cambodia, $275,000 Regional)

- **Capacity building:** PMI will continue to support NMCPs via training courses to build the capacity of NMCP staff.

  a. **Regional:** Skills, such as supply chain management, disease surveillance and reporting, M&E, integrated vector management, and laboratory diagnostic services to quality malaria service delivery will be emphasized. PMI partners will continue to facilitate the ACT Malaria "Management of Malaria Field Operations" course. ($275,000)

- **Field Epidemiology Training Program:** PMI will support trainees from Burma and Cambodia who will focus their field training on malaria prevention and control, including malaria outbreak detection and response activities, and an evaluation of malaria surveillance efforts.

  a. **Burma:** Support for two trainees identified by Burma NMCP officials ($150,000)

  b. **Cambodia:** Support for one trainee identified by Cambodia NMCP officials ($75,000)

COORDINATION

PMI supported the formation and management of the WHO bi-regional Malaria Mekong Program for a number of years, but this office is now closed with the retirement of the previous coordinator and the development of the new WHO Emergency Response to Artemisinin Resistance hub in Phnom Penh. In light of spreading evidence of resistance, WHO/Geneva is playing a larger leadership role in the GMS. At the same time, other donors have increased their support for regional activities, including support for on-the-ground staff in specific areas where resistance has been identified.

Progress to Date:

The PMI continues to maintain its role in regional coordination, drug efficacy and quality surveillance, and M&E. In FY 2012 and FY 2013, PMI provided on-going support for country staff in both Cambodia and Burma. PMI will continue discussions with WHO and other donors to support needed in-country WHO staff in Burma and Cambodia.

Planned activities with FY 2014 funding are as follows ($375,000 total: $375,000 Cambodia):

- **In-country technical assistance and coordination**: PMI will direct its FY 2014 support to the WHO country program in Cambodia. Under the guidance of PMI-supported WHO staff, the country office will facilitate national policy guidance on artemisinin resistance, and provide technical assistance to CNM on national program strategy and policies, strengthening M&E systems and plans (see M&E section) and implementing TES activities (see TES section).

  a. **Cambodia**: Full time support for WHO malaria specialist ($225,000)

- **Cross-border and in-country partner coordination**: PMI will continue to support coordination of malaria prevention and treatment follow-up activities for operational districts in Cambodia with respective neighboring districts in Thailand, Lao PDR, and Vietnam to reach migrant and mobile populations as well as for information sharing activities. PMI will also support efforts to strengthen CNM coordination of malaria partner efforts in both implementation and research in-country.

  a. **Cambodia**: Support for cross-border and in-country coordination. ($150,000)

INTEGRATION ANDCOLLABORATION

With increasing global concern about artemisinin resistant malaria has come concomitant recognition that the GMS requires flexible and closely coordinated approaches that are not limited to single countries. Thailand, for example, cannot eliminate resistant falciparum malaria without working closely with both the Cambodians and the Burmese. The major malaria outbreak now underway in southern Laos threatens Vietnam's malaria control efforts and probably cannot be resolved without intervention from the Vietnamese side. Migratory workers in multi-national companies and along some border areas may be reached more efficiently from neighboring countries than from the countries in which they are working. The WHO has established a regional hub based in Phnom Penh, Cambodia, for its Emergency Response to Artemisinin Resistance; while the Global Fund, also recognizing the need for regional responses, has established a $100million fund for Burma, Thailand, Laos, Vietnam and Cambodia. The PMI coordinates its regional response through the Regional Development Mission for Asia, based in Bangkok. Other key players include AusAID, as announced at an international conference on "Malaria 2012: Saving Lives in the Asia-Pacific," held in Sydney, in November 2012.

Recognizing that it is only one of several regional donors, PMI coordinates closely with others to offer technical leadership, support for filling gaps, and contributions to national and regional strategies. The PMI participated in a joint mission to Vietnam with WHO and AusAID to develop its strategy for management of artemisinin resistance. It coordinates closely with Global Fund, at national levels, regional and global levels and with the Bill and Melinda Gates Foundation.

The PMI continues to support an integrated, multi-disease platform, where appropriate. For example, PMI support to drug quality assessments not only strengthens antimalarial drug quality, but also tests antibiotics and drugs for influenza and tuberculosis. PMI recently supported an assessment of antenatal care specifically around malaria in pregnancy. The report of this assessment has generated several specific proposals, as seen in the Malaria in Pregnancy section of this MOP.

Lower Mekong Initiative

PMI embraces the goals of the Lower Mekong Initiative, a multinational partnership among Cambodia, Laos, Myanmar, Thailand, Vietnam, and the United States, established to support integrated sub-regional cooperation among the five Lower Mekong countries. the Lower Mekong Initiative serves as a platform to address complex, transnational development and policy challenges in the Lower Mekong sub-region. Specifically, PMI objectives for the Lower Mekong Initiative include: 1) focusing on malaria and the need to develop and strengthen a coordinated response; 2) prevention and control of counterfeit and substandard medications; 3) fostering regional collaboration to support implementation of the International Health Regulations and regional-level emphasis on surveillance and response; and 4) sharing good practices across GHI initiatives. Furthermore, cross-border and migrant issues are common concerns for both GHI and Lower Mekong Initiative. Burma joined the Lower Mekong Initiative in 2012, ensuring a strong geographic overlap between the PMI Greater Mekong Subregion countries and the Lower Mekong Initiative. PMI supports surveillance and drug quality monitoring throughout the Lower Mekong Initiative region.

USAID Forward

The PMI team will work to further the following Implementation and Procurement Reform objectives:

Increase Use of Partner Country Systems: Government to government (G2G) grants are primarily feasible in Thailand, among GMS countries. While the current agreement ends in FY 2013, some continuation of direct government support may continue for therapeutic efficacy studies and operation of border malaria posts.

Strengthen Local Civil Society: Support to local non-governmental organizations and community-based organizations is one of the most effective means to access difficult-to-reach migrant and mobile populations. The bilateral regional malaria project is designed to make sub-grants to local organizations. Community-based organizations may be particularly effective in BCC, ensuring ITNs reach populations most at need, and facilitating community-based diagnosis and treatment; thus, in FY2012 and FY 2013, PMI allocated $100,000 to support building capacity of local NGOs in malaria control through an Annual Program Statement from USAID/Cambodia.

PRIVATE SECTOR ACTIVITIES

Private sector activities in the GMS can be divided into three broad areas: private practitioners and the private pharmaceutical sector; the private mosquito net sector; and private workplace programs.

Collaboration with the private practitioners and the private pharmaceutical sector
Cambodia has been doing extensive work with the private pharmaceutical sector. Several PMI partners are involved with the private pharmaceutical sector. With the new malaria elimination targets, malaria case management in the private sector must be improved. The CNM will provide training and follow-up supervision for early diagnosis and treatment to 4,200 private providers in 20 malaria endemic areas during 2011–2012. There will also be an expansion of the medical detailer program to reach providers and different types of unregistered drug outlets in rural areas.

In Burma, PSI supports the "Sun Quality Health Network," a franchise of licensed general practitioners serving low-income populations. As of December 2012, the network included 901 clinics, located in 177 townships, which were providing malaria diagnosis and treatment. The network tested 345,672 fever cases and treated 93,756 confirmed malaria cases in 2012.

Similarly, the Myanmar Medical Association, with support from Global Fund, Three Diseases Fund, Three Millennium Development Fund, USAID and WHO, has a network of private general practitioners under its project "Quality Diagnosis and Standard Treatment of Malaria". The private general practitioners are being supported with training and logistics to deliver quality-assured diagnosis and treatment of malaria. This is being expanded with the support of Global Fund Round 9 and Three Millennium Development Fund, it is expected that 330 private providers in 113 Townships and 360 Village Health Volunteers in 12 fixed/mobile clinics will be part of the network at the end of 2013.

In Thailand, antimalarials are prohibited in the private sector, and there is minimal engagement of private practitioners and the private pharmaceutical market.

Workplace programs
Cambodia, Thailand and Burma all have experience in developing "workplace programs" for malaria. In Cambodia, PMI works with commercial farms in Western Cambodia to test a model of loaning out LLINs to seasonal farm workers through farm owners. Also in Thailand, under the BMGF-funded containment project, BVBD established a number of partnerships with plantation owners promoting malaria prevention and control amongst migrant workers (e.g. "malaria corners" in factories and workplace BCC campaigns).

In Burma, the International Organization for Migration signed a Memorandum of Understanding with the MOH in 2004 to implement a community-based migration health project in Mon State. The Mon State project provides tuberculosis, malaria and HIV prevention, diagnosis, treatment and other capacity building and health education activities in 76 villages across six townships. This project is funded by the Swiss Development Cooperation and the Three Diseases Fund.

Possibly the most important workplace programs will be related to major development projects, such as the Dawei Deep-sea Port Project, an $8 billion construction project in Tanintharyi State across from Kanchanaburi Province Thailand. Development projects attract a large migrant worker population, often into the heavily forested areas and thus workplace programs for malaria prevention and treatment need to be emphasized.

Progress to Date:
WHO continues to play a vital role in regional coordination, but now through a new regional hub financed by AusAID and the Bill and Melinda Gates Foundation. In FY 2013, PMI provided continued support for WHO country offices in Cambodia and Burma but discontinued support for the Mekong Malaria Program Coordinator and office. PMI participated in Global Fund meetings to establish a $100millionthree-year grant for five countries of the Greater Mekong Sub-Region.

Planned activities with FY 2014 funding: (costs are covered in the case management section)

- **Private sector case management:** PMI will support quality assurance and reporting from private providers in Burma and Cambodia, as described in the case management section.

STAFFING AND ADMINISTRATION

Planned FY 2014Activities: *($1,673,000 Total: $540,000 Burma, $284,000 Cambodia, $849,000 Regional)*

Two Resident Advisors will oversee PMI-supported activities in the RDMA, one representing USAID and one representing CDC. They have office space within the RDMA offices in Bangkok, but are expected to travel widely within the subregion. USAID/Cambodia will share approximately one-third of RDMA/PMI staff costs. In addition, Foreign Service Nationals have been hired to support the PMI team in Bangkok and Rangoon, while an FSN position has been funded in Phnom Penh. To facilitate coordination in-country, one Malaria Advisor is proposed in FY 2014 to support the Burma Mission with management of malaria activities. The PMI team will share responsibility for development and implementation of PMI strategies and work plans, coordination with national authorities, managing collaborating agencies, and supervising day-to-day activities.

The RDMA PMI Resident Advisors are part of a single inter-agency team led by the Director of the Office of Public Health, USAID Regional Health Development Mission-Asia. Both Resident Advisors report to the USAID Mission Director or his designee. The CDC staff member is supervised by CDC, both technically and administratively. RDMA-based RAs and the FSN will spend approximately one week a month at USAID/Cambodia providing direct technical and managerial support and will liaise closely with USAID/Burma as well. RDMA-based technical input will also support regional strategies for surveillance, M&E, operational research, and services for migrants. All technical activities are undertaken in close coordination with national and international partners, including the WHO, Global Fund, UK Department for International Development (DFID), Three Millennium Development Goals, BMGF and the private sector.

Locally-hired staff to support PMI activities in the Mekong will be approved by the USAID Director in the relevant Mission (e.g. RDMA, USAID/Cambodia, USAID/Burma). Because of the need to adhere to specific country policies and USAID accounting regulations, any transfer of PMI funds directly to Ministries or host governments will need to be approved by the relevant USAID Mission Director and Controller.

ANNEX

Table 1A
President's Malaria Initiative - *Burma*
(FY 2014) Budget Breakdown by Partner

Partner	Geographical Area	Activity	Budget ($)
CAP-Malaria	Cross-border Focus Areas	a) Community level engagement to deliver malaria prevention and treatment; b) Collect entomologic data; c) BCC technical assistance for community-level implementation; d) Support strengthening national QA/QC	$2,640,000
CAP-3D PSI	National	Support to private sector in diagnostic and case management	$300,000
CDC IAA/ TBD	National	a) Support development of 5-year National Strategic Plan and M&E plan; b) strengthen M&E reporting from state/regional levels; c) provide technical assistance and data analysis support to strengthen routine surveillance at the periphery; d) LLIN durability monitoring	$200,000
CDC IAA	National	a) FETP support for 1-2 Burmese fellows; b) entomologic surveillance supplies	$160,000
Deliver	Cross-border Focus Areas/ National	a) LLIN/LLIHN, RDTs and ACT procurement; b) Strengthening the pharmaceutical management systems	$1,825,000
MCHIP	National	Strengthening ANC practices around MIP	$50,000
USP-PQM	National	Maintain drug quality surveillance network including strengthening enforcement measures	$50,000
WHO umbrella grant	National	Conduct TES studies	$200,000
TBD	National	2014/15 National malaria household survey	$500,000
Total			**$5,925,000**

Table 1B
President's Malaria Initiative - *Cambodia*
(FY 2014) Budget Breakdown by Partner

Partner	Geographical Area	Activity	Budget ($)
CAP-Malaria	Cross-border Focus Areas	a) Community level engagement to deliver malaria prevention and treatment; b) LLIN distribution; c) Collect entomologic data; d) BCC technical assistance for community-level implementation; e) strengthening ANC services for MIP; f) cross border and in-country coordination	$2,205,000
CDC IAA/TBD	National	a) Technical assistance and data analysis support to strengthen and harmonize routine surveillance and M&E at the national level with CNM; b) help incorporate private sector and community level data for national level use; c) coordinate national malaria M&E work stream; d) personal protection evaluation	$175,000
CDC IAA	National	FETP support for 1 Cambodian fellow	$75,000
Deliver	Cross-border Focus Areas/ National	a) LLIN/LLIHN, RDTs and ACT procurement; b) Strengthening the pharmaceutical management systems	$750,000
USP-PQM	National	Maintain drug quality surveillance network including strengthening enforcement measures	$100,000
WHO umbrella grant	National	a) Support WHO country program to provide national technical guidance; b) Conduct TES studies	$475,000
TBD	National	Net use preference assessment	$100,000
Malaria Care/ PSI	National	Strengthening private sector case management and malaria surveillance data collection	$300,000
Total			$4,180,000

76

Table 1C
President's Malaria Initiative - *Regional*
(FY 2014) Budget Breakdown by Partner

Partner	Geographical Area	Activity	Budget ($)
ACT Malaria	Southeast Asia	a) Coordinate and facilitate training courses; b) Provide microscopy/RDT QA/QC training and accreditation; c) regional insecticide resistance coordination	$365,000
CAP-Malaria	Cross-border Focus Areas	a) Community level engagement to deliver malaria prevention and treatment; b) Collect entomologic data; c) BCC technical assistance for community-level implementation	$180,000
CDC IAA/ TBD	Cross-border Focus Areas/ GMS (3 countries)	a) M&E technical assistance and data analysis support to strengthen routine surveillance; b) strengthen national malaria control program M&E plans; c) national survey technical assistance needs; d) assist with outbreak response	$150,000
Deliver	Cross-border Focus Areas/ GMS (3 countries)	a) LLIN/LLIHN, RDTs and ACT procurement; b) Strengthening the pharmaceutical management systems	$450,000
USP-PQM	GMS (4 countries)	Maintain drug quality surveillance network including strengthening enforcement measures	$200,000
WHO umbrella grant	GMS (4 countries)	Conduct TES studies	$424,000
TBD	Thailand	a) TES sites direct support; b) support for strengthening Thai TES studies; c) direct support to malaria posts/clinics/ border posts	$320,000
TBD	GMS (3 countries)	LLIN/LLIHN distribution cost	$50,000
Total			**$2,139,000**

Table 2A
President's Malaria Initiative - Burma MOP
Planned Obligations for FY 2014

Proposed Activity	Mechanism	Budget Total $	Budget Commodities $	Geographic Focus	Description
Preventive Activities					
Insecticide Treated Nets					
LLIN/LLIHN procurement and distribution	DELIVER	1,125,000	1,125,000	24 townships in Tanintharyi, Kayin and southern Rakhine	Procure 300,000 LLIN/LLIHNs for focus areas to fill gaps and reach special populations including migrants and mobile populations
Community level distribution and promotion of ITNs	CAP-Malaria	450,000		24 townships in Tanintharyi, Kayin and southern Rakhine	LLIN distribution, promotion and BCC in focus areas. Distribution will target stable populations and special populations including migrants and pregnant women
SUBTOTAL ITNs		1,575,000	1,125,000		
Indoor Residual Spraying					
SUBTOTAL IRS		0	0	0	
Malaria in Pregnancy					
Strengthening ANC practices around malaria in pregnancy	MCHIP	50,000		Nationwide	Ensure malaria in pregnancy policy, guidelines are updated across Malaria and MCH programs; Develop BCC materials.
SUBTOTAL MIP		50,000	0		
SUBTOTAL PREVENTIVE		1,625,000	1,125,000		
Case Management					
Diagnosis					
Procure RDTs/ microscopy supplies	DELIVER	400,000	400,000	24 townships in Tanintharyi, Kayin and southern Rakhine	Procure ~600,000 RDTs/ microscopy supplies for focus areas for use by community level health volunteers or workers

Activity	Partner		Location	Description
Training and supervision of RDT/microscopy	CAP-Malaria			Support for focus areas - see case management
Support strengthening national QA/QC for malaria diagnosis	CAP-Malaria	100,000	Rangoon	Support for strengthening national reference laboratory for microscopy and RDTs with technical assistance and training
Support to diagnosis and case management in the private sector	PSI Control & Prevention of Three Diseases Project	300,000		Support expansion of the Sun Quality Network with a focus on quality assurance of case management services
SUBTOTAL Diagnosis		800,000	400,000	
Treatment & Pharmaceutical Management				
Procure ACTs	DELIVER	150,000	24 townships in Tanintharyi, Kayin and southern Rakhine	Procure 150,000 ACT treatments for use by community level health volunteers or workers
Case management at the community level, including implementation, training, and supervision	CAP-Malaria	2,000,000	24 townships in Tanintharyi, Kayin and southern Rakhine	Training and supervision in diagnostics and case management of 800 VMWs and rural health center staff
Support for supply chain management	DELIVER	150,000	Nationwide	Technical assistance in supply chain management to Burma MOH and strengthen coordination on malaria commodities (including pharmaceutical management system, forecasting, quantification, management and distribution of pharmaceuticals and RDTs).
Drug quality monitoring	USP Pharmaceutical Quality Management Project	50,000	Drug quality sentinel sites	Strengthen post- marketing surveillance and strengthen quality control laboratories
SUBTOTAL - Treatment & Pharmaceutical Management		2,350,000	150,000	

Activity	Mechanism	Budget	Location	Description
SUBTOTAL CASE MANAGEMENT		550,000 / 3,150,000		
Behavior Change Communication				
BCC technical assistance for community-level implementation	CAP-Malaria	0		See Case Management and Prevention- Support implementing partners with developing and implementing effective BCC/IEC approaches; adapt materials in local languages; and strengthen interpersonal communication
SUBTOTAL BCC		0	0	
Monitoring and Evaluation				
Surveillance and M&E strengthening	CDC IAA/ TBD	100,000	Nationwide	Updating national strategic plans and national M&E plans; development of a surveillance data management and analysis platform
2014/15 National malaria household survey	TBD	500,000	Nationwide	National household survey (e.g. MIS or DHS) to include intervention coverage and anemia/parasitemia estimates
CDC technical assistance for M&E	CDC IAA	12,000		1 TDY for M&E support
Surveillance				
Therapeutic efficacy surveillance Network	WHO umbrella grant	200,000	10 sentinel sites	Conducting TES studies at 10 sites in Burma; technical assistance; drug policy review
Entomologic surveillance (basic package)	CAP-Malaria	90,000	Sentinel sites and Rangoon	Support for entomological monitoring; insectary support in Rangoon
Entomologic surveillance supplies	CDC IAA	10,000	Sentinel sites and Rangoon	Reagents and supplies
LLIN monitoring and durability	CDC IAA/ TBD	100,000	Sentinel sites	Assessment of physical durability and insecticide retention of LLINs

80

CDC technical assistance for entomology	CDC IAA	23,000		2 TDYs for entomologic support
SUBTOTAL STRATEGIC INFORMATION		**1,035,000**	**0**	
Capacity building				
Field Epidemiology Training Program (FETP)	CDC IAA	150,000		Support 1-2 Burmese fellows to participate in FETP
SUBTOTAL CAPACITY BUILDING		**150,000**	**0**	
In-country Staffing and Administration				
USAID Staffing	USAID	540,000		Malaria advisor, 50% Malaria FSN Burma
SUBTOTAL IN-COUNTRY STAFFING		**540,000**	**0**	
GRAND TOTAL		**6,500,000**	**1,675,000**	

Table 2B
President's Malaria Initiative - Cambodia MOP
Planned Obligations for FY 2014

Proposed Activity	Mechanism	Budget Total $	Commodities $	Geographic Focus	Description
PREVENTIVE ACTIVITIES					
Insecticide Treated Nets					
LLIN/LLIHN procurement and distribution	DELIVER	350,000	350,000	14 Operational Districts	Support for LLINs and LLIHNs (hammocks) for focus areas, filling potential gaps, and targeting migrant and mobile populations
Community level distribution and promotion of ITNs	CAP-Malaria	280,000		14 Operational Districts	LLIN distribution, promotion and BCC in targeted focus areas. Distribution will target migrants in Cambodia. Includes sub-grants to local NGOs to assist with net use.
Net user preference assessment	TBD	100,000			Assess household net use and preferences to guide future procurements
SUBTOTAL ITNs		730,000	350,000		
Indoor Residual Spraying					
SUBTOTAL IRS		0	0		
Malaria in Pregnancy					
Strengthening ANC practices around malaria in pregnancy	CAP-Malaria	50,000			Ensuring collaboration and integration of malaria in Pregnancy with NMCP and Maternal Health Programs; updating training and supervision tools; developing BCC messages
SUBTOTAL Malaria in Pregnancy		50,000	0		
SUBTOTAL PREVENTIVE		780,000	350,000		

Case Management

Diagnosis

Activity	Partner			Location	Description
Procure RDTs/ microscopy supplies	DELIVER	200,000	200,000	14 Operational Districts	~300,000 RDTs and microscopy supplies procured for focus areas for use by community level health volunteers (900 village malaria volunteers and migrant malaria volunteers) with expansion to new operational districts (eastern and northern)
Training and supervision of RDT/microscopy	CAP-Malaria			14 Operational Districts	Support for focus areas - see case management
Quality assurance of diagnostics in the private sector	Malaria Care/ PSI	300,000		Private sector	Improve quality of private sector case management through medical detailing, monitoring and supervision; provision of malaria data to national surveillance system
SUBTOTAL Diagnosis		**500,000**	**200,000**		

Treatment & Pharmaceutical Management

Activity	Partner			Location	Description
Procure ACTs	DELIVER	100,000	100,000	Nationwide	Procure ACTs for use by community-level health volunteers or workers; targeting migrant and mobile populations, and to fill commodity gaps in public and private sector
Case management at the community level, including implementation, training and supervision	CAP-Malaria	1,500,000		14 Operational Districts	Training and supervision of 700VMWs; implement active case detection activities and refresher training
Support for supply chain management	DELIVER	100,000		Nationwide	Technical assistance in supply chain management. Strengthening the pharmaceutical management system, forecasting, quantification, management and distribution of pharmaceuticals and RDTs.

Activity	Funding source	Amount	Target	Description
Drug quality monitoring	USP Pharmaceutical Quality Management Project	100,000	Sentinel sites in 12 provinces	Maintain post- marketing surveillance; Strengthen quality control laboratories; Support national enforcement
SUBTOTAL - Treatment & Pharmaceutical Management		**1,800,000**	100,000	
SUBTOTAL CASE MANAGEMENT		**2,300,000**	300,000	

Behavior Change Communication

Activity	Funding source	Amount	Target	Description
BCC technical assistance for community-level implementation	CAP-Malaria	100,000	14 Operational Districts	Support implementing partners with developing and implementing effective BCC approaches
SUBTOTAL BCC		**100,000**	0	

Monitoring and Evaluation

Activity	Funding source	Amount	Target	Description
M&E strengthening	CDC IAA / TBD	100,000		Technical assistance and data analysis support to strengthen and harmonize routine surveillance and M&E at the national level with CNM; help incorporate private sector and community level data for national level use; coordinate national malaria M&E work stream

Surveillance

Activity	Funding source	Amount	Target	Description
Therapeutic efficacy surveillance network	WHO umbrella grant	250,000	5 sites	Conducting TES studies at 5 sites in Cambodia; technical assistance (P4); and drug policy review by WHO-Bangkok-based Principal Investigator
Entomologic surveillance (basic package)	CAP-Malaria	125,000	3 sites	Support for entomological monitoring; insectary support for Cambodia
CDC technical assistance for entomologic surveillance	CDC IAA	24,000		2 TDYs for entomologic support

Operations Research

Description	Funding source	Amount	Notes
Evaluation of personal protection methods	CDC IAA/ TBD	75,000	Follow on to an FY13 pilot entomology study designed to down select personal protective measures in target populations
CDC technical assistance for operational research	CDC IAA	12,000	1 TDY for OR support
SUBTOTAL M&E		**586,000**	**0**
Capacity building			
Field Epidemiology Training Program (FETP)	CDC IAA	75,000	Support 1 Cambodian fellows to participate in the FETP
SUBTOTAL CAPACITY BUILDING		**75,000**	**0**
In-country Coordination			
In-country technical assistance through WHO Program Officer	WHO umbrella grant	225,000	Provide technical assistance and national strategic guidance to CNM (support to WHO Cambodia IPO)
Cross-border and in-country partner coordination	CAP-Malaria	150,000	Participation in cross border coordination activities and assisting with partner coordination at the national level (e.g. secretariat function)
SUBTOTAL REGIONAL COORDINATION		**375,000**	**0**
In-country Staffing and Administration			
USAID Cambodia Foreign Service National	USAID	84,000	USAID Malaria FSN Cambodia
USAID Regional Resident Advisor	USAID	150,000	1/3 of PMI USAID Regional PMI RA to Cambodia
CDC Regional Resident Advisor	CDC IAA	50,000	PMI CDC Regional Resident Advisor to Cambodia
SUBTOTAL IN-COUNTRY STAFFING		**284,000**	**0**
GRAND TOTAL		**4,500,000**	**650,000**

Table 2C
President's Malaria Initiative – Regional MOP
Planned Obligations for FY 2014

Proposed Activity	Mechanism	Budget Total $	Commodities $	Geographic Focus	Geographic Area Regional $	Thailand $	Description
PREVENTIVE ACTIVITIES							
Insecticide Treated Nets							
LLIN/LLIHN procurement and distribution	DELIVER	300,000	300,000	Regional	300,000	0	Support for LLINs and LLIHNs for focus areas and to fill potential gaps in the region
Distribution Costs	TBD	50,000		Regional	50,000	0	Distribution to the community level
SUBTOTAL ITNs		**350,000**	**300,000**		**350,000**	**0**	
SUBTOTAL PREVENTIVE		**350,000**	**300,000**		**350,000**	**0**	
Case Management							
Diagnosis							
Procure RDTs/ microscopy supplies	DELIVER	50,000	50,000	Regional	50,000	0	Procure ~150,000 RDTs/microscopy supplies for focus areas for use by community level health volunteers or workers
Training and accreditation for microscopy	ACTMalaria	80,000		Regional	80,000	0	Support for microscopy training in the region and maintenance of regional and national slide banks
SUBTOTAL Diagnosis		**130,000**	**50,000**		**130,000**	**0**	
Treatment & Pharmaceutical Management							

Activity	Implementing Partner			Location			Description
Procure ACTs	DELIVER	50,000	50,000	Regional	50,000	0	ACT treatments procured to respond to emergency commodity gaps
Case management at the facility and community level, including implementation, training, and supervision	CAP-Malaria	120,000		Regional	0	120,000	Includes technical support and training and supervision of malaria workers, case detection and follow up of high-risk populations.
Case management and supervision at malaria posts/ clinics/ border posts	TBD	140,000		Regional	0	140,000	Staff/site support for 33 malaria posts and clinics
Support for supply chain management	DELIVER	50,000		Regional	50,000	0	Technical assistance in supply chain management to the region. Strengthening the pharmaceutical management system, forecasting, quantification, management and distribution of pharmaceuticals and RDTs.
Drug quality monitoring	USP Pharmaceutical Quality Management	200,000		Regional	150,000	50,000	Maintain post-marketing surveillance; support to regional investigation and enforcement; build pharmaceutical capacity
SUBTOTAL - Treatment & Pharmaceutical Management		**560,000**	**50,000**		**250,000**	**310,000**	
SUBTOTAL CASE MANAGEMENT		**690,000**	**100,000**		**380,000**	**310,000**	
Behavior Change Communication							

BCC technical assistance for community-level implementation	CAP-Malaria	25,000	Tak, Trat/ Chanthaburi and Ranong	0	25,000	Support implementing partners with developing and implementing effective BCC approaches, including adapting in local languages
SUBTOTAL BCC		**25,000**		**0**	**25,000**	
Monitoring and Evaluation						
Surveillance and M&E strengthening	CDC IAA/ TBD	150,000	Thailand, Lao and Vietnam	150,000	0	M&E technical assistance and data analysis support to strengthen routine surveillance; strengthen national malaria control program M&E plans; national survey technical assistance needs; assist with outbreak response
CDC technical assistance for M&E	CDC IAA	12,000		12,000		1 TDY for M&E
Surveillance						
Therapeutic efficacy surveillance network	WHO umbrella grant	424,000	Laos, China, Vietnam	424,000	0	Conducting TES studies in 3 countries; technical assistance and monitoring visits by the WHO Principal Investigator to all 6 GMS countries; support for drug policy review; convening of bi-annual meeting
Direct TES support to Thailand MOPH	TBD	120,000	9 TES sites	0	120,000	Conduct TES at 9 sites in Thailand as part of the TES network

Activity	Mechanism			Location			Comments
Support for Thailand's TES activities	TBD	60,000		Thailand	0	60,000	Build NMCP capacity to conduct TES in compliance with Good Clinical Practice guidance.
Entomologic surveillance (basic package)	CAP-Malaria	35,000		Thailand	0	35,000	Support for basic entomological monitoring
Regional insecticide resistance coordination	ACTMalaria	10,000		Regional	10,000	0	Regional insecticide resistance meeting
SUBTOTAL M&E		**811,000**	**0**		**596,000**	**215,000**	
Capacity building							
Strengthen NMCP capacity	ACT Malaria	275,000			275,000	0	Coordinate and facilitate regional training courses
SUBTOTAL CAPACITY BUILDING		**275,000**	**0**		**275,000**	**0**	
In-country Staffing and Administration							
USAID Staffing	USAID	639,000			639,000		Support for USAID Resident Advisor, PMI Malaria FSN Bangkok, administrative costs
CDC Staffing	CDC IAA	210,000			210,000		CDC Resident Advisor
SUBTOTAL IN-COUNTRY STAFFING		**849,000**	**0**		**849,000**	**0**	
GRAND TOTAL		**3,000,000**	**400,000**		**2,450,000**	**550,000**	

[i]Ministry of Health. "National Strategy for Malaria Control and Pre-Elimination: 2011-2015," Lao PDR Ministry of Health and World Health Organization, July 2010

[ii]Phetsouvanh R, Inthirath I. "Malaria in Attapeu: Situation and Control Measures," Department of Disease Control, 2012 (Powerpoint Presentation – Unpublished)

[iii]Deyer, G "Malaria Outbreak in Attapeu Province: November-December 2011," Center for Malariology, Parasitology, and Entomology and World Health Organization, Jan 2012 (Unpublished written report)